LIFE ON THE

DEEP END

Living with Chronic Illness

Deborah K Steen MS, LPC

Inkception Books

Pain, that cannot forget
Falls drop by drop
Upon the heart
Until in our despair
There comes wisdom
Through the awful grace of God.

Aeschylus

This book is dedicated to my family, friends, doctors, and nurses who have cared for and supported me during my life on the Deep End. A special note of gratitude to my loving husband, Bill and my two daughters, Jennifer and Amanda, whose talents, patience, and commitment made possible the publication of this book.

CONTENTS

Part One

THE BIG PLUNGE

Part Two

BACK TO THE SURFACE

Preface

In the following chapters of this book, I have attempted to describe how I personally dealt with an elusive illness that struck in the prime of my life, that arrived abruptly and yet tenaciously, and that consistently defied an accurate diagnosis for almost three decades. I will share my story of what it was like for me, a young mother of two, to transition in one day, from the "land of the healthy" to the "land of the chronically unhealthy." This book is also a tribute to all those other strugglers, who like me, have been forced, by chronic illness, to set up residence in this "foreign land." I also salute the family and friends who support them and the doctors who daily go "the extra mile" to provide them with care. Finally, and most importantly, I want to share how I believe that God worked in all of it not only to provide strength for the journey, but to create an entirely new and exciting path for me to follow.

Part One of this book describes The Big Plunge, explaining my personal response to an illness that had weakened my body, threatened my self-esteem, and challenged my spirituality. In Part Two, I will share how God helped me achieve acceptance through the people, medical resources, and coping skills He sent my way. Also in

Part Two, I will continue my story about how I dealt with the issue of faith and healing and will review how others have dealt with this issue in their own lives. When I look back on the many books I have read about coping with chronic illness, the ones that seemed to help me the most were the ones that included details of symptoms and diagnoses. When I read about how others were experiencing some of the same frustrations that I was at the time, I didn't feel quite so unusual. This is the reason I have chosen to share the details of this journey in the hopes that others can identify with these patterns of problems and frustrations and, in turn, realize that they are not alone in their struggles.

Introduction

My first inkling I was not immortal came in 1957 when my family traveled across the state and stayed in a hotel. On this typically broiling summer afternoon, my mother, who harbored no great affinity for water play herself, finally gave in and allowed my younger brother and me to swim in the hotel pool.

I was then about six-years-old with a two-year-old brother. Due to my mother's own fear of water, my brother and I had no experience with even the most basic rules of swimming. I, myself, didn't want to let my head get under the water. However, the thought of splashing on top of the water sounded like great fun to me.

Mother worked out something of a compromise to accommodate her own apprehension as well as our desire to have a good time with all the other kids. She equipped each of us with a kiddy-sized inner tube, which she assumed would keep us safe for a splash in the shallow end of the pool.

Seeing other kids with similar types of inflatables bobbing up and down in the kiddy-pool, I thought this was the way to get wet without having to put my face in the water. I eagerly joined in the play. I toddled out to the hot, wet cement, with the colorful plastic doughnut bouncing happily beneath my arms. Easing myself carefully into the cool, blue-green liquid on the shallow end, I joined the ranks of toddlers half my age. Many of them dove off the side into the pool and swam to the other side with ease. My bare feet touched the rough bottom of the shallow end of the pool. I breathed in the competing scents of chlorine and suntan lotion.

Bringing my knees up to my waist, I let the plastic ring support my weight. How much fun this was at first to bob gently up and down, with the cool water beneath me and the sun above graciously warming my face and shoulders. I began to enjoy paddling and splashing along with the other kids.

Eventually, however, my early success splashing and cavorting in the shallow water soon became a bit dull. It didn't take me long to become bored with the baby end of the pool. I saw kids, who were only a few years older than I, jumping off the diving board on the other end into the deep water. That's where the big kids swam.

I pulled myself up out of the water and looked around. My younger brother and his toddler antics distracted my mother from watching me. Emboldened with a false sense of security the inflatable ring provided me and motivated strongly by a desire to swim like the big kids, I bravely toddled over to the other end of the pool. Without another thought, I climbed up on the diving board and jumped off into the deep water.

The next emotions I remember are shock and surprise that I had not bounced off the top of the water as I thought I would. Instead, I plunged down into the inky darkness towards the bottom of the pool. By the time my feet touched the bottom, it seemed to my six-year-old brain that hours had passed, when, in truth, it had been only seconds. At this point, I became completely disoriented. I didn't know which way was up. It looked like a blue-black darkness had devoured me.

Could this be happening to me? I felt so betrayed by that stupid ring of plastic. It should have kept me floating safely on the surface as it had in the shallow pool. But it didn't. Where was it, anyway? Was it still around my waist?

Just when I almost gave up altogether, I saw a sparkle of milky light that appeared to be coming from the wrong side of the pool. That couldn't be the way to the surface. It seemed like the wrong direction for light to be coming from. Some force I couldn't identify seemed to be pulling me towards the light, but I didn't sense myself going up at all. It seemed to me I headed towards the side instead. Now all I thought of was getting back to the air again.

After ignoring my own faulty sense of direction, I soon felt my head breaking through the water's surface wildly. I splashed and coughed and gasped and then went under again. When I came back up the second time, I tried calling to my mom, but the noises from the other swimmers drowned out my water-logged petitions.

At last, someone noticed me struggling frantically and pulled me up out of the water. After coughing a few times, I cleared the water out of my lungs. My mother came running over to me with a towel. She never saw me jump off the diving board and go under or she would have reacted more quickly to help me. I came close to drowning, and it was the first time I can remember feeling totally helpless and overwhelmed by circumstance.

Unfortunately, these feelings returned in my adult life. Thirty years later, as a young wife and mother of two young daughters, I awoke one morning with my first severe flare of inflammatory arthritis. During the challenging months and years following this initial episode, I felt many times the sense of drowning once again-- only not by water. The intractable pain, ever-evolving symptoms, fatigue, depression, and doubts about my ability to cope submerged me. This, for me, was the inevitable beginning of my life on the Deep End.

Part One

The Big Plunge

THE END OF THE SHALLOW END

END

A Day in the Shallow End

I grew up and became the wife of an engineer and a mother of two young girls, one an infant and one a toddler. After college and three years of teaching, I was now a full-time mom and loved every minute of it. We had a three-bedroom house in Broken Arrow, Oklahoma. To me, this time with the girls was precious. I loved taking them places, such as movies, live stage shows for children, swim lessons, and amusement parks. We worked on reading vocabulary starting at age two. By the time they were three, they could each read thirty or forty words from flash cards.

Today I planned an urban safari for me and the girls walking all over the Mall shopping for Christmas gifts. Mandy, the youngest, sat in the stroller. Jenny, fifteen months older, perched on a pillow on the basket behind the stroller. The girls' heads, one blonde and one red, bobbed and twisted as they strained to take in the colorful decorations. My steps kept pace with a jazz rendition of Jingle Bells in the background. While I broke a cold-sweat, the girls squealed and pointed at Santa's workshop in the distance. We all laughed as I accelerated and maneuvered around the rumbling crowd.

The girls seemed to be enjoying the festive mood of the lower level. Wheeling past a twenty-foot Christmas tree decorated with ruby-colored ornaments and golden ribbon, the stroller-for-two wove in and out among the hurrying shoppers. After kids' meals at the Food Court, we found our way to Santa's Workshop and took our place at the back of the long and winding line. Happily, I took the opportunity to catch my breath and pointed to all the lights decorating the tree and the railings around the North Pole set-up. The girls gaped like hungry magpies at the magical Christmas scene. After we waited for a long time, we took our turn for pictures with Santa. I first helped Jenny into his lap.

"What's your name, Little Girl?" began Santa.

"Jenny," she piped while tugging on his beard.

"What do you want for Christmas this year?"

"A Cabbage Patch doll that looks like me," she answered.

"OK, I'll make a note." As Santa's gaze met mine, he smiled and winked.

He then helped Jenny climb down, and I put Mandy in his lap. Shrinking amid the folds of crimson velveteen, she looked a bit intimidated by the bright red suit and shiny black shoes. She, too, tugged on his beard, and it almost came off. After they smiled for pictures, I put the girls back in the stroller.

We then waved goodbye to Santa. I pushed the stroller to the edge of the tiny Christmas winter land scene and took my checklist out of my purse. I wanted to make sure that we didn't forget anything. Making circles around line items, I marveled at the amount of shopping we had done. How long had we been here? I saw darkness through the sky-lights of the ceiling. Had we been shopping for five hours? I decided that was a good stopping place; time to go home.

For the first two years after Mandy was born, the girls and I covered lots of territory with that converted stroller. When I got tired in those days, it was a natural tired, a tired which I felt I somehow earned by the goals accomplished and by the smiles on the faces of my girls.

Trusting God came to me more easily during these brighter days, because every struggle I encountered I could push through. I had no idea how much I relied on my own energy and determination to create happiness for myself and my family. It was easy to see God's blessings in my life, because I worked hard. If something needed to be done, I just pushed on ahead and got it done.

Early Symptoms

During the early years with my husband, Bill, and my daughters, I never imagined the devastating impact a virus could have on my health or even on my life. In the winter of 1987, Bill experienced a relapse of the mononucleosis from his college days. Sometime before his symptoms first presented, he passed it to me. I became ill about a week after him.

I came down with what I considered the worst cold of my life coupled with overwhelming fatigue and memory problems. Frequently, my mind went blank in the middle a sentence. I expected these symptoms to resolve themselves. After little to no improvement within a few weeks, I finally went to the doctor.

He entered the exam room with a stack of papers clipped tightly to the chart. He flipped back and forth between the top three pages. After a minute, he looked up at me through his bifocal glasses that had slid to the edge of his nose. He looked intentionally serious to impress upon me the importance of what he was about to say.

"Your tests showed positive for mononucleosis, and your liver enzymes are elevated five times above normal," he said. He sat as a form of punctuation. "You also have double maxillary sinusitis. Here is a prescription for some strong antibiotics." He decisively tore the paper then handed it to me. "I want to stress to you that this is no ordinary sinus infection," he said as his brow furrowed.

"It isn't?"

"No, this infection is quite pervasive. Take these antibiotics, but if you don't feel better soon, I want you to call me, so we can try a stronger drug."

Confusion followed me as I left with the prescription and the resolve to knock out this infection. If this had spread so pervasively, why not just give me the stronger prescription now and finish it?

Furthermore, it baffled me that something as simple as a sinus infection elicited this intensity from him. What about the mono or the liver enzymes? Would they fix themselves?

A few weeks later Bill recovered from his relapse, and we thought I had as well. I was still extremely tired, but the brain fog had lessened. A follow-up mono spot test came back negative, and the antibiotics cleared up the sinus infection.

One evening, while Bill worked on his hobby sailboat project, the girls and I settled down to watch The Wizard of Oz. I popped a big bowl of popcorn, and we huddled together in front of the TV. We watched as Dorothy retreated from the storm outside into her bedroom only to have her house drawn up inside the swirling winds of a Kansas twister. A few minutes later the same farmhouse landed with a thud. When she went outside, she found a strange world, unlike the Midwestern farm country she called home. Her quest now became finding her way back to Kansas again.

When the movie ended, I put the girls to bed with good-night hugs and went to bed myself. My mind rehearsed all the things I planned for the next day. I just knew things would now return to normal.

The First Dive

As the morning sun filtered in through the curtains, I opened my eyes to a flood of aching throughout my body ten times more intense than ever before. I thought I must have come down with a bad case of the flu. When I tried to sit up, instead of hopping out of bed as I usually did, my body stalled as though caught inside some invisible vise. I tried to move my arms and hands to support my torso while I pushed off from the bed. As I did so, I noticed stabbing waves running from my shoulders through my arms to my fingers on both sides of my body.

What on earth was wrong with me? After finally working my way into a partial standing position, my knees felt weak and wobbly under the weight of my torso. My feet, too, were sore and tender.

Later, when I went into the bathroom, I gawked at my hands and protested, "I can't believe these are my hands!" They looked like stuffed sausages, especially the knuckles. The mid-joints were red and swollen and painful. In fact, many of the joints on both sides of my body appeared warm, red, swollen, and stiff. It seemed that somehow during the night I had been transformed into a ninety-year-old woman.

Everyday actions became instantly alien. I limped down the hallway to the kitchen. Gritting my teeth through the stabs, I hooked my thumb under the knob of the cabinet. I stared up at the medicine. Even if I could reach the aspirin bottle, how was I going to be able to push and turn through the child safety cap? I had now plunged into the murky water of the Deep End of the pool again.

After this flare of acute pain and sudden loss of normal movement, mainly in my hands and feet, I returned to the doctor.

"Your labs all came back normal, but it is obvious something is wrong. I'm giving you a prescription for Voltaren, a drug to help with the discomfort and the swelling in your joints," he told me.

"What do you think is wrong with me?" I asked.

"I think there is a chance you have some type of arthritis, but since the lab tests are all normal, I can't tell you what kind you have." He then looked puzzled. "However, I want you to see if this medicine helps you. If it doesn't make you feel better in a week or two, then call me, and we'll try something else. I'll check you again in three months to review how you are getting along."

As I left his office, my disappointment for not getting a firm answer and my confusion about the normal test results created a mental cyclone tumbling in the back of my mind. I need my old body back, but if that can't happen, just please, someone, give me a name for what is wrong! How can I feel so bad while nothing shows up in the labs?

I took the medication as prescribed, and after a few months, it did seem to reduce the joint inflammation but did nothing at all to help the flu-like aching. Most of my joints still refused to bend as normal. To top it off, every morning I struggled with about three hours of stiffness before I could coax my body into something that could in the least resemble normal movement.

At this time, my illness invaded our home like an uninvited guest. This new intruder hobbled in on two legs – pain and fatigue. Although I tried to go on with our routines, this interloper soaked up so much of my energy, I could only accomplish a fraction of my daily tasks. Due to pain, I moved more slowly, and the fatigue demanded periods of complete rest throughout the day. If I denied myself this rest, in a stubborn refusal, the illness punished me with more pain. With enough time, it robbed me of the wife and mother I wanted to be. Jenny recognized that something different about Mommy. She knew me as someone who played games in the backyard with her and went on picnics at the lake. Mandy, on the other hand, only knew her mom as a broken person. Yet, both girls grew up with much uncertainty in their lives due to the vacillating nature of my symptoms. I fought heavy negotiations with my body to fulfill as many of our family plans as possible.

For two years, I made regular trips to the doctor every three months. Each time the doctor told me I might have some type of arthritis. He ordered blood work which always came back as normal. Despite the negative lab results, my symptoms persisted and worsened. How could I hurt like this and have nothing show up in my labs?

What's in a Name?

In February 1989, I saw Dr. Ellen Zanatakis, an arthritis doctor (rheumatologist), for the first time. As I waited for her to come into the exam room, I noted the medical degrees and specialty certificates on the wall.

When she walked through the door, she smiled, introduced herself, and reached out for a hand-shake. I braced myself for the impact of the squeeze on my joints. Instead, she delicately supported my hand and pressed my red, spongy digits with the slightest pinch. She released my hand and requested me to touch the tip of my fingers to the thumb of each hand. Many of them would not bend that far. She also asked for me to bend my larger joints, such as wrists, knees, and elbows. None flexed with a normal range of motion.

"I'm ordering labs and x-rays, but I don't need to wait until they come back to diagnose your illness," she said. "It seems obvious to me you have rheumatoid arthritis (RA). You see, about 40% of the time in its early stages it will present with negative lab results."

Stunned, I couldn't believe how quickly she knew.

"I want you to stay on the Voltaren, and we'll add Prednisone as well."

"Whatever you say," I replied.

She then spoke more deliberately, looking squarely into my eyes.

"You need to accept the fact your illness is incurable, and you will take medicine for the rest of your life. It will be hard for your family and friends to understand what you are going through, so I would recommend you contact the Arthritis Foundation. They provide lots of information on your illness and on services they provide in the community."

Sitting in the exam room, while she went for pamphlets and wrote prescriptions, I saw the diagrams of bones and the cut-away display of the joint, surrounded by the bursa. It illustrated the bursa in an RA patient expanding with fluid and inflammatory cells. According to the display, if the disease is left untreated, these cells can, in the later stages, cause joint erosions and deformities.

I thought of what this diagnosis meant to me and my family. Suddenly my relief in having a name that validated my symptoms morphed into a fear that my life would never be the same as it used to be. The worst-case scenarios came instantly into my mind. Would it cripple my hands and feet? Would I end up in a wheelchair? I then imagined a healthy me, playing volleyball or icing a birthday cake, or hosting a child's birthday party. Would I ever be able to do these things again?

On the way home from the doctor's office, I remembered my older sister, Shirley's medical problems. She had been diagnosed with something called rheumatoid pneumonia a few years before my problems began. I wondered how her condition related to mine. Along with inflammatory arthritis, Shirley experienced chronic kidney problems and bleeding stomach ulcers. She found herself in and out of hospitals for over thirty years. She had taken early retirement from her job and currently remained home-bound. This frightened me. Could I prevent this illness from robbing me of my life goals?

In the weeks following this original diagnosis, I tried to find as much information on the illness as possible. I contacted the Arthritis Foundation and requested educational pamphlets. I learned rheumatoid arthritis is a type of autoimmune disease. It is caused when a person's immune system goes rogue and attacks her own body. Doctors recognize many types of autoimmune disease, but they do not always occur together. There was no way to know how my disease would progress compared to my sister's.

I was quickly concluding that everything about my life now was going to be different. Mornings used to bring renewed vitality; now they brought pain and stiffness that lasted for hours. During other parts of the day, I did everything I knew to try and coax my body back into productivity. Later in the evening, I would crash. Sitting with a heating pad, I would coax the throbbing joints back to rest, so I could sleep better at night. Would I ever find a medicine that could make this pain go away?

Of Maladies and Medicines

Next came the first year in the Decade of Overlaps. I found my problems didn't end with one diagnosis. Several others came along for the ride. One morning I awakened to find my eyelids sticking together. It was difficult to pry them apart. As I pulled the lids opened, it felt as though my eyes were filled with sandpaper. Even watering them down with Murine eye drops was little help. I went to the bathroom to see if I had something in them. I only noticed red streaks. This lasted for days until it was time for my follow-up appointment.

"You are too young to have that much trouble with dry eyes," Dr. Zanatakis told me. "And you are not on any medication that can cause dry eyes. I want to send you to an eye specialist for a dye test to rule out something called Sjogren's syndrome."

A few weeks later I was sitting in an exam chair and having something red put in my eyes. The eye specialist described the test he was doing.

"This is called a rose Bengal dye screening to find out if you show any abrasions on your corneas. If you do, this will be a positive reaction signifying Sjogren's."

"Does this relate to the RA?" I asked.

"Well, yes, it can," he answered.

He began the test. After staining both my eyes, he examined them through his special magnifier. My eyes stung from the dye.

"Yes, I see corneal abrasions on both eyes," he concluded. "Here is a pamphlet about Sjogren's and a sample of some artificial tears I want you to use in each eye four to five times daily." I hoped this medicine could end the chronic feeling of sand in my eyes.

I brought the eye report with me when I saw the rheumatologist again.

"According to your eye specialist," she said, "your test results indicate Sjogren's syndrome. It can affect either the eyes or mouth or both."

"I have only had problems in my eyes," I told her.

"Yes, I know. I'm prescribing another drug called Plaquenil.

Although it may reduce the eye inflammation, it can also damage the retinas. You should have regular eye exams as long as you are on it to make sure you are not developing a toxic reaction to it."

The good news was this drug was effective in treating my dry eyes. The bad news was its potential toxic side-effects.

Another problem developed that same year. One day I had been polishing furniture. I noticed the inside of the pointer finger on my right hand turned a dark purple from the mid-joint to the tip. The only way to get the normal color to return to this finger was to submerge it in warm water for about twenty minutes.

I finally knew something was wrong when, on another cold winter day, I had been leading a community class at the public library. After the meeting ended, I saw black smears all over the inner side of my fingers on both hands. Since I had been using a black dry erase marker during the meeting, I decided these stains came from the marker.

"Hey, you've gotten black marker all over your fingers," said one of the group members.

"Yes, I guess so," I said. However, when I tried to wipe the black off with a paper towel, there was no black left on the towel. Puzzled about this, I pulled on my gloves and drove home. To my surprise when I got home and pulled off the gloves, the black stains had gone away. What on earth was going on with my hands now?

"What you're describing sounds like another overlap condition to the RA called Raynaud's phenomenon," my rheumatologist explained at my next appointment. "It affects the circulation in the hands and feet predominately."

"What next?" I demanded, feeling perplexed at the litany of diagnoses attaching themselves to the original one.

She handed me a prescription.

"This is Procardia, a medicine that should improve the circulation in your hands," she offered.

I took the Procardia and from the first week, my hands grew warmer and stronger. Although I complied with my doctor's instructions, the overlap conditions in my diagnosis continued to increase as did the size of my medical records chart. I fought no less than two major sinus infections each winter and spring, each of which required four rounds of antibiotics to eliminate. To top it all off, Dr. Zanatakis next sent me to an ear, nose, and throat specialist (ENT) for an evaluation of chronic ear ringing.

The ENT insisted the ear ringing was caused by my arthritis medication. He told me I would need to decrease the dosage. He then stared at me rather curiously.

"Do you know your nasal septum is broken?" he asked me.

"Not really," I answered.

"Well, it is," he replied. "I think if we can rebuild your septum, your sinus infections will decrease dramatically."

"You're talking about surgery, right? You see, I don't want to do that now. With everything else I'm dealing with, cosmetic changes are not high on my priority list," I told him.

"No, of course not," he agreed. "But I believe if we complete this surgery, you'll see a great reduction in the number of your sinus infections. However, it's your decision to make."

With all my health issues to consider, I would never have considered surgery for cosmetic reasons. Yet fewer infections did sound better to me. "Well, if you think this will help keep me well?"

"I believe it will," he assured me.

A few weeks later I had the operation. At the post-op appointment, the ENT debriefed me on the procedure.

"Your septum was not only broken, but splintered, and many of the splinters were embedded in the walls of your sinuses. I removed the fractured pieces of the bone and cartilage and used your own tissue to reshape your septum."

"Will this help prevent more sinus infections?" I asked.

"Yes, certainly," he said.

At this point, I, as well as my doctors, believed the sinus problem was separate from the autoimmune disease. In time, however, this would not be so certain.

A New Drug

By the summer of 1990, my rheumatologist told me my illness was becoming more severe. She prescribed low-dose Methotrexate, a type of chemotherapy often used in low doses with moderate to severe RA. After my first week on the drug, I took a mental note of my own pattern of response. If I took the medication on Thursday, I was nauseated all day Friday. But by Saturday, my nausea had disappeared. I would gladly sacrifice one day of nausea for six other days of better functioning.

After about three months, I eventually achieved my first symptom-free day since 1987. I would never forget that beautiful, brisk, October day. I was able to rise out of bed, shower, dress, and do my chores without having to wait for my body to get into gear.

That afternoon, I walked out onto the front porch. I gazed at my front yard. My two stately elms seemed to be calling to me. These elms, along with the other trees on the street, were parading their brilliant leafy tapestry of golds, reds, and browns for one last time this season. Soon the harsh winter winds would begin to denude their branches and cover them with snow.

I took a deep breath of the crisp, clean air. Without pain, the whole world seemed new. I felt so blessed to witness nature's beauty that time of year after my first morning without pain in about four years.

Deep Water Again

I had discovered medicine could indeed make a difference not only in my pain level, but also in how well I functioned throughout the day. The Methotrexate helped with both. I could now lift a heavy pan filled with water and carry it to the stove without cringing. I could put my daughter's hair up in a ponytail without my fingers stiffening. I could even scrub the floor, vacuum, and lift a load of laundry without my hands throbbing for the rest of the day.

Unfortunately for me, however, these improvements did not come without a price. After a few more months on Methotrexate, a different problem arose. Although my joints were almost back to normal, my muscles soon became the major problem. The joint swelling, stiffness, and pain were now replaced by muscle pain and extreme leg weakness. By dinnertime, each evening, the backs of my legs throbbed with severe muscle spasms. At times the weakness even made it difficult for me to push down on the gas pedal when I drove.

When I saw my rheumatologist again, I told her about the muscle spasms and the leg weakness.

"I'm going to prescribe a tens unit for the spasms," she told me. "Whenever the spasms begin, you can put the electrodes behind your knees and turn on the unit. I'm also sending you to a physical therapist to evaluate the leg weakness and to a nutritionist to evaluate your weight loss and decreasing muscle mass."

She was right about the weight loss. I only weighed 101 pounds. Although I thought I was eating normally, I had now lost more than forty pounds in only a few months. When I saw the nutritionist, she saw how atrophied my leg muscles were. Her response was to put me on a high-fat, high protein, muscle-building diet. I couldn't believe what her dietary recommendations were for me.

"I want you to drink three milkshakes per day in between your meals," she directed, sounding something like a top-sergeant in the army. "Milkshakes, not milk. I also want you to eat fatty meats like ribs and roast rather than lean meats and to eat gravy on your meat when you can."

"That doesn't sound very healthy," I told her.

"It's what you need to strengthen your muscles," she said.

I couldn't believe I was hearing this from a certified nutritionist. Nevertheless, I did try to implement these changes into my diet. I wanted the strength back in my legs again, and I wanted the spasms to go away permanently. I felt my body had betrayed me again. I was trying to do the right things to take care of myself. It didn't seem to matter. I felt angry with myself for being weak. In my mind, my physical weakness paralleled a weakness in my character. I considered myself to be a strong person, not this weak one that was now getting only weaker.

My rheumatologist gave me the name of a physical therapist and scheduled an appointment for me on the following week. Her office resided in a converted townhouse. On the first floor were rooms for support groups and community education in one wing and medical offices in the other. Both floors of the upper level had been turned into a health library.

At my appointment, the therapist told me, "Your leg muscles are not firing properly. Because of the spasms and the weakness, you present with what to me looks like multiple sclerosis (MS)," she announced. I didn't want to believe my ears. Another overlap?

"I will send my report to your rheumatologist," she continued. "For walking, I am recommending you use a metal cane with a flat handle which is perpendicular to the ground. This type will give you more stability, which is what you need." She also gave me muscle-strengthening exercises to do at home.

Although I exercised regularly, the weakness continued to worsen. I was then attending a warm water aerobics class at the YWCA. My leg muscles weakened to the point I needed help to get out of the pool. "How much more of my self-esteem will this illness take from me?" I thought, completely mortified.

Then another symptom arrived on the scene. One evening I awoke from my nap and discovered the whole left side of my body was numb. When I touched the left side of my body with my right hand, I felt as if I was touching a corpse. Within a few hours, this numbness episode resolved. I had by this time become experienced in dealing with chronic pain. However, now I was learning the absence of sensation could be even more frightening.

When I saw the rheumatologist again, she agreed with the physical therapist. "Your primary care doctor and I agree on a diagnosis of MS."

I protested. "The Raynaud's and the Sjogren's, I can accept. They sort of make sense to me. But MS is a totally different condition, isn't it?"

"Well, MS is in the same family of conditions as connective tissue diseases like RA," she explained. "However, MS affects the lining of the nerves instead of the joints. That's why I'm sending you to a neurologist."

The neurologist insisted on doing an arteriogram, an MRI, and other neurological exams to rule out MS and other neurological complications.

"I agree with your other doctors who think you may have MS in addition to the other issues," the neurologist told me.

However, my mind just wouldn't let me believe this could be true. I didn't want to presume I knew more than this specialist and my other clinicians. Yet I believed it was important for me to be candid with her.

"I don't think I have this condition. It just doesn't make any sense to me," I said.

She countered my feeling with a fact. "MS is an autoimmune disease. It's entirely possible you could have both RA and MS."

Realizing the doctors knew more about these conditions than I did, I scheduled the neurological tests, which, in time, all backed me up; they all were negative. For me, this settled the matter.

I finally noticed something curious about this period of overlaps. With every secondary diagnosis, I felt as though I was losing another part of me--of the Me I had been, of the Me now, and of the Me, I still wanted to be in the future. How could I get Me back again? Until I did, I knew I would continue to feel defective, thinking my experience was unique. I wondered how many more things could possibly go wrong with my body. I knew there couldn't be many people who had this number of secondary conditions complicating their original diagnosis. I certainly identified a radical shift in my own self-image. I not only felt flawed but also felt guilty about being flawed. I could no longer imagine myself as highly energetic and productive. With each additional syndrome or overlap condition, the troublesome doubts haunted the back of my mind. What did I do to deserve this?

Although the tests showed normal results, my doctors were still insisting I go to Mayo to rule out MS. Perhaps if I went, we could eliminate this diagnosis once-and-for-all. Because of this possibility, I decided to go for the consult. After registering with Mayo Clinic, I was instructed to go off all my medications three months before coming. After following their instructions, an amazing thing happened. When I stopped the Methotrexate, all my muscle symptoms disappeared. It was wonderful! My joint pain and leg spasms resolved as well. I could walk without a cane.

I thought my doctors would be as excited as I was by this news of remission. Nevertheless, the doctors still wanted me to go for the Mayo consult. Thus, in the winter of 1991, my husband and I left for Rochester, Minnesota.

A Chilling Day

Mayo Clinic conducted a variety of neurological tests which came back negative. That eliminated the MS diagnosis. However, I was sent to be tested for Raynaud's. Thus, on a bitterly cold February morning, I entered the Mayo Clinic Vascular Lab. It had been snowing outside, so my fingers were already numb and tingling.

"We're going to be doing a cold-water immersion test for Raynaud's phenomenon," one of the lab technicians explained. "We'll need to first take individual blood pressure and temperature readings on all ten of your fingers before the immersion and again after to see how long it takes your finger temperatures to recover."

I suddenly spied the tiny blood pressure cuffs, which resembled blood pressure cuffs for dolls. These same cuffs were hooked up to some sort of monitoring device on which both the pre-test and post-test pressures would be recorded.

After the technicians completed the pre-test pressures and temperatures, one lady wrinkled up her forehead and whispered to the other technician, "I'm not sure we should perform this test on her. Her baseline readings are so low, we may permanently damage her hands."

The technicians resolved to go ahead and perform the ice-immersion test. They took both of my hands and submerged them in the ice water. I can't remember exactly how long they were submerged, but it seemed like hours. I can't describe how painful this was. On a scale of 1-10, where 1 is the lowest level of pain and 10 is the highest, I think this rated a 10.5. With time, numbness replaced the pain. After my hands came out of the ice water, the pain returned. It took them much longer than normal to recover, but I was fortunate since they did progressively return to a temperature a little below the baseline. One of the technicians then reported the results to me.

"I think we can safely say you have Raynaud's. No doubt about that," she said.

When I returned home from Mayo, my rheumatologist put me back on the Procardia for the Raynaud's. I thanked God the MS diagnosis had now been put aside permanently. One less diagnosis to add to the growing list.

A New Ally

Not long after I returned from Mayo, my primary care physician left to practice in Arizona. For someone with a chronic illness, especially if it's a complex case, changing doctors is demoralizing. It's sort of like digging another hole before you can build a mountain. There is no way the new doctor can easily or quickly absorb and process this type of complicated health history, which is the product of perhaps a decade or more of interactions between the medical team.

This is especially true for the person who has a complex illness within a setting of negative labs. Because of this, in my early days of dealing with this chronic problem, I often felt I had to be my own defense attorney at each office visit. As the physician stared at the negative lab reports and at my myriad of reported symptoms, it was my responsibility to make my case showing the clinician why they should take me seriously.

One day my new doctor, Dr. Lane, said, "You know, I see many other patients with rheumatoid arthritis, and none of them have all these problems together." She was smiling as she said this but avoiding eye contact. It amazed me that she was holding a chart with notes written in black and white from other doctors certifying these overlapping conditions, yet she remained skeptical. If she couldn't believe me, couldn't she at least believe them?

"I guess I'm just an exception to every rule," I joked, trying to cut through her obvious doubts with a bit of humor. I knew she was just echoing the same incredulity about these overlaps as I had been harboring in my own mind.

I stuck it out with this doctor. I understood the cyclical nature of my symptoms, and I knew that with enough time, she would see it firsthand. When clinical signs in my body did appear, which she could see and recognize as abnormal, she reformulated her skeptical first impression of me. We developed a solid rapport, and she did not ask me to repeat any of the tests unnecessarily. In fact, while I was still struggling to resurface from the Deep End of the Pool, Dr. Lane became one of my most loyal allies.

HITTING BOTTOM

Only the Nose Knows

One cold winter morning, I experienced the strangest symptom of all. My nose hurt with an aching and grinding pain as if my arthritis had relocated there. I examined my profile in the mirror. If I didn't know better, I would have thought I had broken my nose again. The bridge did not appear as straight as it did after my last surgery. I could feel the crackling soreness in the lining of the nostrils as well.

A few weeks later, the ENT examined my nose and sinuses. "I see your nose has deviated again," he said. "There are also obstructions in your sinuses, called granulation tissue, that we can remove. But first we need to do some nasal biopsies and an ANCA blood test to rule out a condition that can be related to your RA called Wegener's granulomatosis." He pulled out a pen and began writing on the chart.

"I've never heard of that, what is it?" I asked, breaking the silence.

"It's a type of vasculitis or inflammation of the blood vessels that sometimes attacks the nose and sinuses. It can be very serious. That is

30

why we need to do the biopsies. It often presents along with RA symptoms. It can be life-threatening if it moves from the nose and sinuses to other organs. However, it can also be disfiguring even if it remains confined to the face. That's why it's important to catch it early."

Several words stood out from the normal din of medical jargon I was used to hearing. I had dealt with possibilities of deformities, with serious symptoms, and of course, with inflammation. Yet, I could not wrap my mind around the possibility of a life-threatening condition. How could Wegener's granulomatosis spread to other organs? Which organs?

About a week after completing the biopsies, when I went back in for my post-operative appointment, I hoped the pathology report would soon put the Wegener's diagnosis to rest at last. Such was not the case. At the post-operative exam, I asked the surgeon about the biopsy report. Looking a bit confused, he told me he would need to check on it.

"If you'll wait here a moment, I will go and call the lab to obtain the report over the phone," he said. He left the room to make the call. A few minutes later, he returned. "I'm afraid the pathology report is positive," he told me. "You definitely have Wegener's."

I was in shock, not expecting this outcome at all. This new level of diagnosis came at the worst time. During my partial remission, I decided to go back to school for my master's degree in counseling psychology. From recommendations of colleagues at the Arthritis

Foundation, this sounded like the next step forward from my time as a successful support group leader. I sat on the exam table recycling the words "life-threatening" and "spreading to other organs". Could anything be done to stop it or postpone it?

"So, what do we do now?" I asked.

"I will need to consult with your rheumatologist about treatment," he said.

We ended the appointment with less conclusion than I expected. I marveled at the lack of certainty in my doctors. Whatever disorder was operating inside of my body surprised even the specialists; none predicted this. Could there be a viable treatment for a disease that changed its mind?

Later that evening the classroom was crowded with students who were hoping for an easy "A" in this undergraduate class, entitled Abnormal Psychology. The instructor entered and took her seat in the desk at the front of the room.

"Would someone volunteer to hand out the syllabus?" she asked. A student on the front row accepted the challenge. "As you can see from the syllabus," she said, in a rather firm tone of voice, "attendance and participation are two very important parts of your grade in this class. You need to be here at every class, and you need to make sure you keep up with your reading assignments. If you miss more than one class, you can't expect to make a good grade."

I thought how shallow the threat of a bad grade in psychology was compared to a diagnosis of Wegener's. How could anything ever again be more important than getting my health back? I discovered how distracted I was from what the teacher was saying. If I ever wanted to move on with my life, I needed to find a way to separate these two areas. Certainly, other people made paths through chronic illness to achieve their life goals. I decided to keep my attention on studies in class and focus on health issues at another time.

Then on a Sunday evening, several weeks later, I received an unexpected call. I had been at home recovering from a flare of my symptoms. Finding it impossible to distract myself from the nasal pain, I had been trying alternating hot and cold packs when the phone rang. After I picked up the receiver, I heard the ENT surgeon's voice on the other end of the phone.

"Did I tell you that you had Wegener's?" he asked.

"Yes, you did," I answered.

"Well, you don't," he stated matter-of-factly. Completely floored, I remained silent while my mind tried to keep up with what he was saying to me. I should be utterly relieved I was being told I didn't have this serious condition. However, right then, all I could grasp was the absurdity of it all.

"Then why did you tell me I had Wegener's in the first place?" I asked, suddenly fighting to suppress indignation. I thought about the stress of the last two weeks Bill and I had been through.

"It was a mix-up with the lab when I tried to obtain the results over the phone," he said. "When the written report came in, the actual results were negative." He continued, "Now you can check back with your rheumatologist and go from there."

"Of course, this news is wonderful--an answer to prayer," I told him. I suddenly remembered my care group at church had been praying for me that same evening. Amazingly the Wegener's diagnosis had been totally reversed. Oddly enough, I continued to feel numb inside.

Beyond the Name Game

I began having problems sleeping, remembering things, and making decisions. I sensed a type of despair not felt before this. Always before, I held on to hope things would eventually resolve – the more I learned about the autoimmune disease, the better I could cope. However, after the Wegener's diagnosis had been added to the long list of other diagnoses I had accumulated already, my mind and emotions became totally overwhelmed. This was the treadmill I had found myself on since 1987.

However, there finally came a time when I grew so frustrated with this mind game I decided to accept the fact I may never know what the definitive diagnosis was for me. I decided to set a limit on any new testing; beginning at my primary care appointment.

"Doctor, I don't care what name or names to call what's wrong with me," I said. "I'm just tired of spending so much time in doctors' appointments and in tests that aren't telling us anything. We both know I have some sort of autoimmune disease. And we have a treatment for it that seems to be helping. That's why I'd like to try to cut out all the extra tests and specialists and just come to see you when I need to."

Dr. Lane smiled, and her eyes widened. "Well, that's OK if the treatment would be the same," she explained. "However, different illnesses sometimes need different treatments. That's why it is sometimes important to have the right name."

"I understand, but I just want to go on with my life even if I don't know the exact name. I also want to call a moratorium on further complicated and expensive diagnostic tests that aren't giving us any new information."

"You have been through a lot of tests," she admitted.

I began to think I was making some headway in this discussion.

"I just feel right now I need to focus on school and my family and pray my symptoms will not interfere with my life goals. In my mind, I have an important choice to make. I can let this illness keep me from accomplishing my dreams, or I can jump off the diagnosis treadmill and take my life back again."

"OK, since your medications seem to be working well for you, we'll keep the referrals to a minimum for now, if that's what you want."

I felt as though a weight had been lifted.

"I believe it's what I need," I said. "I'm having trouble sleeping, making decisions, and concentrating because I just can't escape all of these things going wrong with my body."

She tilted her head to the side. "Maybe you're depressed."

"Me . . . depressed?" I barked out with all the righteous indignation I could muster. "You don't understand. I'm an extremely positive-thinking person. I've spent the last few years reading positive psychology books . . . I'm a support group leader, and everyone tells us we have one of the most positive groups in the community. . . I can't be depressed."

"It can happen." she countered. "Going on the symptoms you've just described, I think it is a good possibility." she insisted. "Why don't you make an appointment with a counselor sometime this week?"

I wanted to resist this with other arguments, but she was right. I was in graduate school to become a therapist. If I could tote the positive benefits of counseling to others, why should I reject them myself? Even though I believed I was not depressed, it might be nice to hear it confirmed.

Depression: A New Kind of Bottom

Soon after, I found myself sitting in the most serene office imaginable. Comfy couches with throw pillows, trickling water of the fish tank, and the indirect light from table lamps created a very homey environment. I thought how easy it would be to fall asleep in here. This counselor spoke with ease and a quiet tone. She asked me simple questions about my experiences with family, friends, and doctors.

Then, she posed one insightful question on the depression screening inventory. "Do you believe things will eventually get better for you?"

I thought about what my honest answer would be.

"Well, if you had asked me that question five years ago, or perhaps even a year ago, I could have easily given a positive answer," I told the counselor, "but right now, in this setting, because of the Wegener's scare, I honestly cannot say, 'yes,' to that question."

I was shocked to hear myself say that, especially after all the positive books I had read, and after all the positive lectures I had given myself.

"I need to be honest with you," I continued. "Right now, at this moment in time, I cannot see things getting any better."

The counselor leaned towards me.

"And why is that?" she asked.

"I can only see more of the same . . . more overlaps and wild-goose chases for a diagnosis that will somehow make sense out of all this chaos. Right now, at this moment in time, I don't think that will ever happen."

The counselor asked again, "You don't think things will ever improve?"

After having more time to think, I answered even more emphatically.

"No, I don't."

The lady squared her shoulders as she sat up straightly in her chair.

"So, you are getting your counseling degree?" she asked.

"Yes," I answered.

"Then you probably have studied about depression. Right?"

That was an easy one. "Yes," I replied.

"Then you should also know sleep problems and difficulty concentrating and in making decisions combined with a feeling of hopelessness sounds a lot like depression. Right?"

I thought through this for a moment.

"Wow... I really am depressed."

It was one thing to read about depression in books. It was quite another to see it in myself. How ironic it was that while I was studying about depression in class, I was losing my own hope in a better tomorrow and didn't make the connection.

One by one, the obstacles had come to my finding the Surface. It was getting hard to believe in the possibility of ever finding it. I fought for years to maintain a positive outlook all on my own, but I arrived at a place in which I needed additional support. How could I give myself a hope that defied my actual experience?

A few months after this session, a new doctor ushered me into his office. He then came over and shook my hand and introduced himself to me. After glancing at my records, he looked up.

"You have been through a lot," he said. "Would you like for me to pray with you?"

"Of course," I replied. I was surprised at his request but felt honored he wanted to do this for me.

After he finished praying, he asked, "Have you prayed for healing?"

"Many times," I told him. At this point, I began to feel this was becoming more of an interrogation rather than an office visit.

He looked me squarely in the face and asked, almost in an accusatory tone, "Then why aren't you healed? Jesus tells us if his child asks for bread, he will not give him a stone. Or if he asks for a fish, he will not give him a snake." He was quoting Matthew 7:9 from the Bible.

I was speechless. I couldn't believe what my ears were hearing. This doctor had taken a beautiful passage of scripture and weaponized it. His words felt like knives stabbing me in the heart. Was he implying I'm not good enough to be healed or I'm not a child of God? I could now feel the hot tears welling up in my eyes, but I was determined not to break down in front of this doctor. Somehow, I waited patiently for him to finish speaking and conclude the appointment. I hurried out the door and to the parking garage. Then I couldn't hold the tears back any longer.

As my car slid down the busy streets, the stoplight ahead turned red. I was trapped in my billowing thoughts, which blew into my mind like the storm surge of a raging hurricane. How many times had I driven down this street after a doctor's appointment with few answers that made sense to me? Now, this doctor had me questioning my faith. What else would this illness take away from me? First, I lost my energy and mobility. Next was my emotional well-being, and now my spiritual assurance. . . what would be next?

Without a doubt, I had now hit the Bottom of the Pool again, but this time, it wasn't my body or my emotions which had been compromised. It was the very core of who I was as a Christian which had been challenged.

STILL IN OVER MY HEAD

A Call Worth Answering

The stoplight ahead turned green. As my car slid through the busy city streets, the stormy thoughts about what the doctor had told me kept recycling through my brain. Suddenly, out of nowhere, a comforting notion floated in to stem the tide of negative thinking. If only I could talk to Marvin, the minister at my church.

As I pulled into my driveway, the thought kept echoing inside my head. At last, I made it to my front door and opened it. As I walked into the house, I heard the phone ringing. I rushed to answer it.

"Is this Debbie? How are you doing?" Marvin said. "Something told me you might need to talk to me."

I couldn't believe it, because he had never called me before this. I explained to him what had happened at my doctor's appointment and what the doctor had told me.

"I don't believe God's answer to our prayers is always a 'Yes,'" he said. "Remember when Paul prayed three times for the thorn in his flesh to be taken from him? God answered, 'My grace is sufficient for you,' right?" He quoted II Corinthians 12:9.

Considering this reference to the Apostle Paul, I remembered more and more passages from Scripture that describe hardship. I concluded that more important than instantaneous miraculous healing is the faith we develop in waiting for God's deliverance. At that moment, I knew that God was reminding me that He was working in my situation for some greater purpose. I was not responsible for the healing. I simply needed to turn to Him for the strength to endure whatever happened.

Therefore, for the next seven years, I continued my graduate studies and my career and focused not on what I had lost, but on what remained in me for God to use. He was faithful to bring me the right support at critical times, like this one, including my counselor, my doctors, my friends, and family.

By 2001, I had recovered from depression and had completed my master's degree in counseling psychology. I found myself working as an outpatient therapist in a Christian psychiatric hospital and using all the skills that I had learned to help people manage mental illness.

A New Diagnosis

One day in the Mall, I walked by a store window. The display featured three lava lamps, with jets of multi-colored liquid flowing rhythmically upward. I watched the ease and regularity with which the blue, green, and red bubbles swirled gracefully to the top of the lamp. Yet, as soon as they hit the surface, they plunged just as quickly to the bottom again.

As soon as we found one treatment for my illness, invariably something would come along and submerge me back to where I began. At times, side-effects from the medications created disorder within my body, and I would need more medicine to combat the side-effects. Also, the disease process itself kept changing its mind about where it would show up. On top of this, sometimes treatments would simply stop working as if my body were adapting to them.

"The mouth and skin sores are typical symptoms of another condition called Behcet's disease," Dr. Zanatakis told me. "This condition is rare and does often include joint symptoms much like rheumatoid arthritis."

"You mean, I don't have rheumatoid arthritis?" I asked.

"You'll be glad to know Behcet's disease is much less likely to cause joint erosions or deformity," she explained. "As a matter of fact, many people with Behcet's present no joint symptoms at all."

"Then this condition is not as serious as RA, right?"

"Usually not as severe joint involvement," she replied. "However, it can manifest some serious complications at times. Especially if there is eye disease, which is one of the most severe complications. It can even cause blindness."

"The only problem I have in my eyes right now is the Sjogren's," I told her.

"No, but your skin lesions are significant," she replied.

"Well, yes, I suppose so," I said. I then remembered the first mouth sores that occurred years ago right after I returned from

Mayo. At first, I didn't even mention them to my doctors, because they were not painful. They just looked like dark purple blisters, but they disappeared quickly, so I just felt they were not important.

"What about my joint and muscle symptoms," I asked. "Do these problems occur with Bechet's?"

"Yes, Bechet's can cause joint and muscle inflammation, and is often misdiagnosed as rheumatoid arthritis for this reason."

"Why didn't any of the lab tests I've had over the years pick it up?"

"That's one of the problems with Behcet's," she explained, "It's an extremely rare disease, and there are no lab tests which can specifically diagnose it. At times, the labs are completely normal or may show results typical for some other type of inflammatory arthritis. I would like for you to think about trying a new type of drug called Enbrel. It's been used successfully in Behcet's. Here is some information on this medication. Take it home and read about it and let me know if you want to start it at your next appointment."

During the next few weeks, I read everything I could find on Behcet's and the new drug, Enbrel. The information I gathered confirmed that blindness was one of the most serious complications. Since Plaquenil successfully managed the Sjogren's, I decided I would wait to start the Enbrel until I believed my health issues made it worth the risks. Enbrel came with a long list of potential side effects since it essentially suppresses your immune system. This list included the possibility of such things as tuberculosis, fatal infections, certain types of cancer, and neurological disease. I thought it would not be worth the risk unless my symptoms became unmanageable with my current treatment.

The Red Eye Initiative

One night a few months later I awoke suddenly in the middle of the night with both eyes stinging and feeling unusually warm. I got out of bed and went to the bathroom and looked in the mirror. Shocked, I saw both eyes filled with blood, with no white left in them at all.

After bathing them with a cold cloth, I went back to bed. By morning, they were much better than before. Although they were still red, the stinging had gone away. By the end of the day, they had returned to normal.

Then a week or two later, I felt a sharp jabbing pain in my left eye. It felt as if someone stuck me in the eye with a hot needle. When I looked in the mirror, I noticed just the inner corner of the left eye was filled with blood.

The frequency of these episodes continued to increase over time. At first, the eyes burned and remained red only a short time. However, the more I used my eyes, the more often the red attacks occurred. I also noticed the red eyes came the day after a flare in my muscles or joints. During some of the episodes, the corner of the eyes would become red, with what appeared to be a reddish string of inflammation running right down the center of the reddened portion. This type of red attack lasted much longer, perhaps a week, before the eye cleared again. Because these symptoms were not always present when I went to my doctor appointments, I took pictures of my eye symptoms to my eye doctor and to my rheumatologist at my next follow-up appointments.

When she saw these pictures, my rheumatologist told me she was concerned. She came over and sat down beside me.

"I think you should think seriously about starting a biologic drug called Enbrel, because, as I told you, Behcet's can cause a serious type of eye inflammation, and if not treated properly, it can result in blindness."

I sat there silent. My mind visualized a set of scales. On one scale sat the word blindness; on the other scale were the words dangerous side-effects. I felt betrayed by my own body.

"Bechet's can progress quickly in the eyes," she told me. "If left untreated or without effective treatment, you can lose your vision very quickly."

I left the doctor's office carrying with me her warnings about Behcet's in the eyes. After arriving home, I made a cup of tea and situated myself in a quiet, comfortable spot. I needed to decide about this treatment. I battled the fear I would make the wrong decision, and it would be too late. I would either lose my vision or develop drug-resistant tuberculosis or something else even more deadly. The problem was I wouldn't know whether I had made the right decision.

Trying to narrow down to a solution, I remembered how the Methotrexate brought my first remission. The worst side-effect was the muscle weakness which led to the threat of having MS. Was the remission worth the risk of side-effects though? Was that beautiful pain-free day in autumn as well as the following months of pain relief and improved daily functioning coming later worth my walking with a cane and going to physical therapy for a short time? Yes, I believed it was. Could preserving my vision be worth the risk of even the worst of Enbrel's side-effects?

After several more months of red eyes and blurriness when fatigued, I decided to go ahead and try the Enbrel. Every two weeks I injected a dose of the medication. Almost immediately, I saw an improvement not only in my eyes, but in my joints, skin, and muscles. The whites of my eyes were no longer injected with red streaks. The bleeding in my eyes had stopped as well.

However, within a few months, I began experiencing recurrent infections requiring multiple rounds of antibiotics to resolve. Infections in individuals with suppressed immune systems spread quickly and can be life-threatening. I knew this was important to address with my rheumatologist.

She referred me to a newer medication called Humira and a corneal specialist. Before trying another biologic, I wanted to get the Enbrel out of my system and see if the inflammation would return to the eyes.

"It appears you have mild episcleritis which has been helped by the Enbrel. You also have mild Sjogren's which is well-managed with the Plaquenil," the eye doctor told me at the first appointment. He then continued, "You will need to return every six months for us to check for side-effects from the Plaquenil. Although it is rare, at times, this drug can affect the retinas of the eyes and, if not caught in time, can cause blindness."

How ironic that now my choices appeared to be possible blindness from the Behcet's or possible blindness from the Plaquenil.

"So, for now, everything is under control?" I asked him.

"Yes, but we need to monitor your Behcet's in the eyes very carefully. I'm giving you some steroid drops for the inflammation in your eyes."

"What is your opinion about me starting the Humira?" I asked him.

"I believe your eye inflammation is mild right now, but with Behcet's, it can get worse very quickly. I tend to agree with your rheumatologist. It might be a good idea to start the Humira."

Because of the risk of more infections and because my eyes were still doing well, I delayed starting the Humira. I wanted to get more information on the Behcet's before I made my decision. I'd been told I had rheumatoid arthritis, MS, and Wegener's in the past. Now I was told I don't have any of these conditions. Maybe I don't have Behcet's either. The infections I experienced from my months on Enbrel cautioned me against using another biologic.

From my research on the American Behcet's Disease Association's website, I learned that the foremost Behcet's treatment center in the United States at that time was in New York City. Its Director, Dr. Yusuf Yazici, was also the Assistant Professor of Medicine at New York University's Hospital for Joint Diseases. In May of 2008, Bill and I arrived at Dr. Yazici's office for a second opinion on the Behcet's diagnosis. I had mailed my records ahead of the appointment, so, after listening to me explain my past and current symptoms, he presented his conclusion.

"I think since your main problem right now is joint pain, you have more of a seronegative rheumatoid arthritis picture than one of Behcet's," he said.

All I could think of was the myriad of other problems I experienced in addition to joint pain.

"My inclination would be to treat you as having rheumatoid arthritis," he added. "However, even if it is Behcet's, I would probably treat you with Humira or another TNF inhibitor. Thus, my recommendation would be to use Humira as the next option, being careful about infections," he said.

This consult left me feeling utterly baffled, but I knew I would have to start a new treatment plan. I obviously didn't have a straightforward case of anything, but both were treated with the same medicine. That settled it. At my next follow-up session with my rheumatologist, I requested a prescription for the Humira.

FOLLOW THE LIGHT

Surf's Up

The white-capped waves rolled gently in onto the gray sandy beach at Monterey Bay. Bill, Mandy, and I had come to Monterey to visit Jenny, who was in Naval language school at a facility nearby. Today the sea appeared to be in a good mood. Its gently-rolling surf lapped at the beach much as a mother's gentle hand caresses the brow of her child.

I strained to imprint this placid scene in my mind because waves are not always this gentle. At times they are angry monsters devastating the shoreline and flooding cities and towns with their torrential assault. When the cooler ocean air meets the warm coastal waters, the waves grow wild with their rage. Soon the surge grows higher and more destructive. How do humans cope with such a threat?

Like the Enbrel, the Humira treatment remediated my inflammatory symptoms throughout my body. No more flu-like aching, joint swelling, lesions, or red-eye attacks. But also, like the Enbrel, it left my body vulnerable to waves of infections. Since our bodies are exposed to a variety of micro-organisms daily, I didn't need to contact sick people to develop an infection. Even the garden-variety bacteria that are supposed to be inside the body, can outgrow their welcome when the immune system doesn't keep their numbers down.

At first, I expected a certain amount of this. Imagining the waves rolling in as a normal part of my new life on the Humira, I was not surprised. Yet, when the frequency and severity of these waves began to increase to the levels I had experienced with Enbrel, I paused treatment. I hoped that, like the Methotrexate, there might be some lasting effects of the medication that would keep the disease at bay and give me some time in between storms to work with my doctors to find a new treatment.

Because Dr. Zanatakis's office stopped taking my insurance, I was forced to change rheumatologists. I sat in the office of my new specialist, Dr. Debbie Gladd Foley, trying to explain to her why I stopped the biologic.

"The Humira's really helped me," I told her. "I feel so much better than I did before taking it. My joint pain is much improved. Especially my hand pain. I've even been able to do some heavy gardening and landscaping again. My eye inflammation seems to have gone away altogether, and my Sjogren's is being managed well with the Plaquenil."

As I told her this, I thought this sounded like a strong case for staying on the drug. I then added, "But the problem is I've been having one infection after another. I just get through taking one round of antibiotics and then I require another one. This is the reason I feel I need to go off all biologics for a while."

The doctor looked at my chart. She asked about specific dates of recurrent infections.

"It does look as if we should try you on a non-biologic due to the infections," she concluded. We agreed I would try another type of anti-inflammatory drug. She then prescribed a drug called Imuran.

The Tidal Waves Roll In

One day in mid-December, after I had been off the biologics for around three years, I developed a severe pain between my left eye and the top bridge of my nose. Recently recovered from another sinus infection, I had been on two rounds of Cipro. By now, I was accustomed to headaches and sinus pain, but somehow this was different. I fought the pain all day with Tylenol, Benedryl, hot and cold compresses, and by accessing pressure points, which sometimes helps me reduce the pain of migraines. This time, nothing seemed to work. Finally, one of the hot packs gave me some relief, and I fell asleep for the night.

Early the next morning, when I awoke, I was elated to find the pain had disappeared. However, when I went into the bathroom and looked in the mirror, I saw my left eye was swollen and bulging a bit. I immediately called Dr. Morrel, my current PCP. She instructed me to go to the acute care clinic in Broken Arrow. She called ahead and got me an emergency appointment. I hesitated to drive with the eye in this condition, so my daughter Jenny drove me.

The doctor at the clinic saw me immediately. She walked into the exam room and took one look at me. Without taking my symptoms or history, she referred me immediately to an ophthalmologist. By the time this doctor examined me, I could not even look up. She sent me directly to the Emergency Room at Saint John's Hospital in Broken Arrow. Now my left eye bulged noticeably. After sending me to radiology for a scan of my eye, the ER doctor told me,

"You have a large mass behind your left eye and your ethmoid sinus. Are you in any pain?"

"No, no pain at all right now," I answered. He gave me a puzzled look.

"I think it most likely you have orbital cellulitis. This can be quite dangerous, so we are going to call in a specialist from the main hospital in Tulsa. You try and relax as much as you can while I go and call him."

A few minutes later, the ER doctor returned.

"He told me to keep you here. He wants to come and see you. This condition, you see, is very rare, and neither he nor I have ever seen anyone with this."

I suddenly felt as if I were on display in some exotic fish tank. Nevertheless, I thanked the doctor for his help as he dashed out the door again. I knew the weather outside was rapidly getting worse, with both ice, sleet, and darkness making the rush hour on the roads a challenge for the best of drivers. Finally, the doctor came in again.

"Change of plans," he said. "We've decided to send you to Tulsa in an ambulance. I've already made the arrangements."

I was thinking all this was happening so fast I couldn't process it in my mind. About that time, my husband, Bill, who had been out of town on business, came into my room. I told him what the doctor said to me. He told me some friends from our church were praying for me and for my doctors. A few minutes later I was wheeled out on a gurney to the ambulance and then driven to, as the doctor had called it, "Big Saint John's."

Soon they were wheeling me on a gurney through the halls of the main hospital downtown. I stole a look at myself in a mirror in the hallway. I was taken aback by my appearance. Not only was my eyeball bulging, but now my eye bled beneath the skin on my left cheek. The bleeding left an ugly purplish bruise which covered the upper left quadrant of my face. I could not believe all of this was happening while I felt nothing- no pain at all. I thought everyone who saw me being wheeled in looking like this would think I was a victim of domestic violence.

After I was settled in my room, Bill and my daughter Mandy came to stay with me. Jenny needed to get home to her children, who were now out of school. A few minutes later, two of my surgeons, Dr. Chad Chamberlain, an eye surgeon and Dr. Chad Putman, an ENT surgeon, came by to brief me on what they had planned to do for me. Both told me this was a very acute and serious situation. They wanted to be frank with me and my family.

"This appears to be something called poly-orbital cellulitis," explained Dr. Chamberlain, "and the mass is large, about the size of your left eyeball." He then continued, "We need to go in and remove the mass because it is definitely life-threatening. However, the operation, itself, also carries a high risk for brain injury or death, because the membrane separating the orbit from the brain is extremely thin and delicate. If the infection or inflammation or even a surgical instrument penetrates through that membrane, death or permanent debilitation could be a result."

The question of the day was: Should I choose the surgery and risk brain injury or death, or should I refuse surgery and wait for whatever it is to burst behind my eye? To me, the decision was relatively simple. Although the doctors warned us most people don't survive this type of surgery, I knew we had to get that mass out of my eye. I then signed the surgical release forms and waited for what would happen next.

A Light at the Bottom

Although I realized I should have been frightened by now, I sensed this warm blanket of peace wrap around me! I had never felt like this before. Something inside me knew that everything was going to be all right. I recognized this kind of peace was not something coming from myself. It was certainly not coming from my mind. I believed that it must be coming from God and that it must be a result of others who were praying for me.

I then heard voices in the hall outside my door. Suddenly the door opened and in walked Clem Witt, the leader of our community group at church. Clem walked up to my bed and asked me if he could pray for me and my family.

"That would be wonderful, Clem," I answered.

He then prayed a beautiful prayer asking for healing and for peace for me and my family. He told me there were many others at our church who were praying for me as well.

Early the next morning, on the way to surgery, we stopped off for one more CT scan.

"Yes, it's still there," the eye surgeon said. "This scan looks just like the first one."

Amazingly, the peace I had felt earlier remained just as constant now while I was on the gurney as it was before in my room. They wheeled me into the operating room and soon all went black.

The next thing I remember is being back in my room on the floor and being surprised I was still alive. Dr. Chamberlain came by to check on me. We could tell he was relieved but a bit confused.

"I'm not sure how to explain this. We couldn't find the abscess," he said. "I went all the way back to bone looking for it, but we couldn't even get enough material to establish what type of microbe might be involved. I have brought in an infectious disease specialist, Dr. James Hutton, the Director of Infectious Diseases here at Saint John's. You are an interesting case for him. You will be his only personal patient. He'll be coming by to meet you sometime soon. In the meantime, how are you feeling? Are you in any pain?"

"Not too much," I answered. "The pain pills seem to be working."

"How's your vision?" he asked.

"I have some double vision, but I can see OK."

Later Dr. Hutton came by with an entourage of interns and residents, who seemed eager to see not only a patient who had orbital cellulitis, which is rare; but who also survived the surgery for it, which seems to be even rarer still. The nurses clued me in about Dr. Hutton. They said he was the best infectious disease doctor in the whole city and the Director of Pathology at the OU Medical Center in Tulsa. I stayed in the hospital for three days, and each day I could set the clock by Dr. Hutton and his retinue of aspiring clinicians.

"Since I had no surgical sample to determine what type of microbe might be responsible for the abscess (if it were a pathogen, that is), I decided to prescribe wide-spectrum antibiotics to make sure the abscess didn't return," he explained. "I am putting you on three of the most powerful antibiotics available. Two administered by IV and one given orally."

Amazingly, I tolerated the drugs well. The only reaction I had was some itching, that was managed well with cold packs.

I was so grateful to God for making the growth disappear. None of my doctors could explain it. It surely was a miracle and an answer to prayer.

Before I left the hospital, Dr. Hutton ordered a PICC line

installed, since he wanted me to be on one IV antibiotic and one oral antibiotic for two more weeks at home. A PICC line is a portal which is implanted in the arm that will carry the antibiotics directly to the heart, so they can be readily circulated to the entire body. He sent us to the Infusion Center on our way home to train us on how to give medication through the PICC line. Admittedly, I opted out of this task from the onset. Bill, as a power plant engineer, was accustomed to laboratory procedures at his job.

For the next two weeks, he and I both lost a lot of sleep. The IV's had to be administered routinely every four hours around the clock. He had the system down pat, flushing before and after every IV. Nevertheless, we were both relieved when two weeks were over.

A few weeks after surgery I went in for my post-operative appointments. One to my ENT and one to my eye surgeon. When I saw Dr. Chamberlain, he took a picture of my left eye. He told me to use an antibiotic cream for a certain period.

"Your left eyelid has dropped down because of the surgical trauma," he explained. "To help correct this, we will need to perform eyelid reconstruction surgery."

"You mean I will need more surgery?" I asked.

"Oh, it's just a very simple procedure," he told me. "We have an outpatient surgical wing right here at our offices. You can go home the same day. It's not a big deal." he insisted.

To me right then everything was a big deal. My body was exhausted from the strong antibiotic therapy and I hated the idea of more surgery.

"It will make all the difference in how wide open you will be able to get that left eye," he said. Then he went over to his desk and retrieved his laptop. On the screen, he pulled up a picture of the CT scan prior to my surgery. He showed the scan of the growth to me. "It was the size of your eyeball. None of us can explain why we were not able to find it," he added.

"Know what I think," I said. "It was a God-thing."

"I tend to agree with you," he said.

"What do you think caused the problem? My ENT thinks it was caused by a blocked sinus. What do you think? Was it caused by infection or by inflammation?" I had put him on the spot, but I wanted his opinion.

"I am more prone to think it was the autoimmune disease," he answered. "You see, when I cut through it, I found some abnormal tissue . . . it was more. . . friable than normal."

"So . . . you suspect the Behcet's or the Sjogren's?"

"Yes, I do, and I want to make you a copy of your CT scan before surgery," he added. "I think you should take it to your other doctors, especially to your rheumatologist and to your eye doctor to let them see just what it looked like before surgery." He then copied the digital copy of the CT scan on his machine and handed the paper copy to me.

Two months later, I returned to Dr. Chamberlain for the corrections on my left eyelid. Everything went smoothly with this last surgery, and, over time, my eye continued to open wider.

When I went back to Dr. Gladd Foley, she told me, "I think it might be the Behcet's that caused the cellulitis in your eye," she said. "I strongly encourage you to go back on the biologic." I decided to listen to her. Thus, in March of 2014, I started back on the Humira after being off of it for about three years.

Breaking Through

After years of confusion and frustration, God answered this prayer for healing in a dramatic way. I once believed I could only reach the Surface if I could find a cure or if God would heal me. Next, I decided it would be when I no longer experienced chronic pain. Now, after much prayer and meditation, I realized it could only be accomplished by my breaking through my own stubborn will for my life and surrendering to the plans God had for me. Sick or well, in pain or not, I now understood God had a purpose for my life, and this was all that was important. Only by giving God this control could I ever learn to find His true peace.

I also realized that my surviving surgery for orbital cellulitis changed me in a most fundamental way. Yes, I certainly came close to death in this situation, but I learned an invaluable lesson from it – that through one's faith and the prayers of others, even at the Bottom of the Pool, God's Light still shines through!

TREADING WATER

In the months that followed my emergency eye surgery, I began to pray that God would give me the wisdom I needed to make good decisions about my healthcare and that He would help me hold on to that peace I experienced in the hospital – a peace that would sustain me even in the most difficult times. As time passed, medications stopped working and needed to be switched. I even found myself in a place in which continuing my work at the hospital was not an option. After working at Brookhaven for fifteen years, I retired and said goodbye to my colleagues and patients. Yet, throughout these changes, I knew that God still had a great purpose for my time left on this earth. I had made it to the Surface and had learned how to Tread Water there.

An Unexpected Undertow

The proof of this change came with my next challenge, a diagnosis of ovarian cancer. On July 25, 2016, when I completed my annual physical with my PCP, Dr. Dana Morrel, she found what felt like a mass when palpating my abdomen. She sent me to a specialist who performed an ultrasound of the mass. It confirmed a growth of 13-by-12 centimeters which was large enough to warrant a CT scan and a referral to a gynecological oncologist. The doctors referred to it as an ovarian tumor. Within a few days, I completed the CT scan. The results were highly suspicious of cancer since they revealed that the mass was organizing its own circulatory system inside itself.

I soon learned that Tulsa only had two gynecological oncologists in the entire Metro Area. I learned I would have to wait five weeks to be seen by one of these specialists. Realizing that ovarian cancer can be rapidly progressive and that my "tumor" was already massive, I researched other cancer treatment centers in the United States. My online research revealed that M.D. Anderson Cancer Institute in Houston had about twenty gynecological oncologists and that this facility was considered by many the foremost cancer treatment center in the United States. I promptly scheduled an appointment for two weeks later. During the weeks before my appointment, I had every reason to be worried and frightened. But I determined I would not let this new diagnosis pull me down again. I decided it was high time I learned how to Tread Water. Once again, I felt the same amazing peace like I felt the last time in the hospital when I had my eye surgery. I prayed every day and journaled my feelings. Something inside me just insulated me from all the negative thoughts about what could possibly be in my immediate future. I was so grateful for this gift.

Bill and I arrived at my first appointment at M.D. Anderson on August 28. It was with a gynecological oncologist named Dr. Nicole Fleming. When I saw Dr. Fleming, she did an exam and reviewed the test results that I gave her.

She looked perplexed. "You definitely have an abdominal mass," she said, "And it's the size of a basketball. I think it was more the size of a soccer ball when these scans were completed. Could you not tell something was different?"

"No, not at all," I answered.

"I'm not happy about having to do the surgery on you that will be required to remove it," she said. "It would be much preferable if we could just do a laparoscopy, but because the mass is so large, it will require a laparotomy."

"Who will be the surgeon?" I asked.

"I will," she answered.

For some reason, I trusted this doctor. She possessed a manner that was determined but was also very compassionate and caring.

"However, because of your complex health history," she continued, "I want you to be seen by one of our internal medicine doctors and have some other scans run. There are basically three possibilities. The first is that it isn't malignant, but benign. In that case, we will just remove it, and that will be all the treatment you will need. That would be the preferable scenario. The second possibility is that it is malignant but contained. In that case, too, surgery would be all you would need for treatment. I will be doing some staging by removing tissue from surrounding areas and sending them to pathology. If they are all clear, then you would not need any chemotherapy. The third possibility is the tumor is malignant, and it has spread to other areas. In that case, you would require chemotherapy."

Bill and I looked at each other. I knew this must be hard for him to take in and process.

"You will see me again before your surgery for a preoperative appointment," the doctor explained. "It will probably be next Wednesday since your surgery is on Friday. In the meantime, you'll be seeing someone from internal medicine, because I need that doctor to sign off on you for surgery."

"So, the next thing I need to do today is labs?" I asked.

"That's right," she answered. She then walked over and took both my hands in hers and looked directly into my eyes and said, "Don't worry, I'm going to take good care of you."

Something about the way she said those words gave me such peace. I knew God had brought us to the right place and to the right doctor to take the best care of me I could possibly have with this problem. Maybe I was, with God's help, learning how to adjust to life on the Deep End. I knew the next few weeks would be rough, but I suddenly had this feeling of peace again wrapping itself around me and keeping all the fear away. Something inside me told me everything was going to be OK.

The Heart of the Matter

The next morning, I went back to the Center for a CT scan of the chest and an electrocardiogram (EKG). I also was scheduled to see the internal medicine specialist, Dr. Sunil Sahai. Dr. Fleming had asked him to review my history to determine whether I could have the surgery to remove my tumor without severe complications.

Looking at my chart, he appeared to be troubled by something, and I could easily sense his feeling of frustration.

"The EKG from this morning shows your heart is under some sort of stress and appears to be enlarged on the left side," he continued.

"Could that be caused by the tumor?" I asked him.

"Well, not really, because it is on the wrong side for it to be caused by the tumor. Have you ever had an abnormal EKG before?"

"Yes, several times, but it was nothing serious, just some abnormal t waves," I answered.

"The problem is there is no doubt you should have the tumor removed, but that is going to put even more stress on your heart . . . we're talking about major surgery to do a laparotomy and remove a tumor so large . . . it's not something I would approve if I saw any other choice."

"So, you're saying you will approve the surgery, but you're not happy about it?"

"Yes, that's the problem. I want a heart ultrasound done, and I want you to see one of our rheumatologists to consult with me on this. I don't feel comfortable making this decision by myself. So, that's what we will do. "

On Friday of that same week, I was scheduled to see the rheumatologist for a second consult. After I arrived in the exam room, he began to ask me questions about my own health history and my family health history as well. I told him about how I woke one morning in 1987, after having mononucleosis, with joint flares on both sides of my body. I explained to him the various diagnoses and false diagnoses I had been given for my symptoms.

"I think, from what you have told me, you have rheumatoid arthritis as well as Behcet's," he said. "There are cases of the two disorders overlapping." He then turned to the current test results including the heart ultrasound. Suddenly he stopped and pulled up the test results on the screen. "The ultrasound was normal," he said.

"Normal? You're kidding." I just couldn't restrain my excitement. "Why do you suppose the EKG showed an enlarged heart? Was it just a bad test?" I asked, then added, "The internist was extremely concerned about the heart issue."

"No, not a bad test, it just sometimes does this," he answered. "Since this test was normal, I'm going to sign off on your surgery, because you need to have this tumor removed."

It was wonderful – a normal heart echo! I looked down at the bracelet my daughter had given me just before I came to M.D.

Anderson. It said, "Trust in the Lord with All Your Heart." No doubt God was behind this outcome. Seeing these sudden changes in the test results overnight uplifted me and allowed me to rely more on that ever-present peace in my heart.

Preliminary Diagnosis

When the morning of surgery arrived, the anesthesiologist told me although the degenerative changes in the neck and spine showed up in the x-ray, my neck appeared to be stable enough for the intubation I would need for surgery. I thanked God for getting me through one more hurdle. Soon they were wheeling me down the long corridor to surgery. The gurney stopped in front of the door, where Bill and his sister, Janet, gave me a hug, and then I was wheeled into the operating room. Within minutes, I was asleep.

When I awoke, Bill was standing over me talking to me.

"The surgeon told us the tumor is malignant. She took out both ovaries, both tubes, and your appendix," he stated, matter-of-factly.

"What else about the tumor?"

"Dr. Fleming took some of the tissue to send it off for a final pathology report," he answered.

"She only could tell us what the preliminary pathology report told her – it was malignant. But . . . she thinks there is a very good chance it is contained. That is what it looked like to her." He seemed very heartened by this last fact.

Answered Prayer

All in all, I had no major problems recovering from the surgery. I was scheduled to return to see Dr. Fleming again in about two-and-a-half weeks for the final pathology report. Despite hearing that the tumor was malignant, we left Houston feeling positive that at least it might be contained and completely removed from my body. No matter what the actual outcome, I knew I could remain content knowing God was working in this situation.

As the next two weeks progressed toward our return trip, I found this post-operative appointment, in some ways, more intimidating than all the others put together. This was because I realized whatever the report was at this appointment would determine my chances of beating this thing which insinuated itself into my life so abruptly – this thing called cancer. I found an opportunity in which I could allow myself to be very fearful. However, instead, I called my church groups and asked them to be praying for me on the exact day and time of my appointment. These stalwart friends had been praying for me all through the years and especially through the surgery. I wanted to know that I would be surrounded by prayer for this next step.

As I sat across from Dr. Fleming at my appointment, I was not sure I was hearing correctly when I heard her say the final pathology report came back with a benign tumor label. It was not cancer! She then showed me a copy of the report and explained it to me as best she could. "Your tumor was benign, showing positive for one cancer marker, but not the three markers needed for a cancer diagnosis," she explained.

I was still focused on the word "benign." My mind parked on that word, taking in all the wonderful difference it made to my life and to the life of my family.

Dr. Fleming then asked Bill to come in to join us and then continued, "According to the report, it's most likely your tumor did not originate in the ovary, but rather from the pancreas or the liver. It did replace the right ovary, but the pathologist believes it was not ovarian in origin."

"How strange. What does that mean, exactly?"

"The pathologist recommends your gastroenterologist scans for any other small tumors that might still be in the liver or pancreas. . . but not right now I would say. However, if they are there, they would more than likely not be malignant, but benign," she explained.

There was that beautiful word again. "So, there will be no need of follow-up treatment?" I asked.

"That's correct," she answered.

"How well are you recovering from the surgery?" she asked.

"Extremely well," I said.

Then Bill asked, "So this means we won't need to come back here again?"

"That's right," she told him. "I would love to see you again, but I'm happy for you that this turned out the way that did. If for some reason, you ever did come back here again, it would not be to see me, since your problem is not gynecological."

"Thank you so very much, Doctor," I told her. "You told me you were going to care of me, and that's just what you did."

Promises Kept

Dr. Fleming had kept her promise and had taken good care of me. When I received the benign diagnosis, I felt I was undeniably the most fortunate person in the world at that moment. How quickly our perspectives can shift! After all, in one hour, I had gone from expecting a long battle through chemo-therapy and negotiating its effects with my other medications, to having the luxury of simply going home.

The great miracle that Christ had accomplished in me was not the reversal of the cancer diagnosis nor of the vanishing orbital cyst. It was not the reversal of the MS nor the Wegener's diagnosis nor the skills I learned from years of living with chronic illness. However, the great miracle was what Christ had accomplished in my heart. It was my facing a terminal illness and knowing with an unshakeable faith that I could trust His Spirit to give me peace. I then knew, no matter the number of nor intensity of the waves that would come, I could Swim on the Surface of the Deep End of the Pool.

Part Two

Back to the Surface

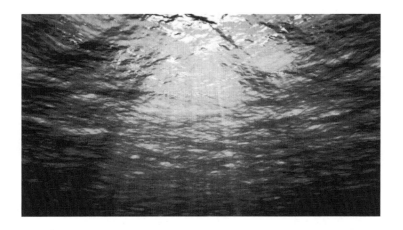

PUSHING OFF FROM BELOW

The Team Really Matters

Years before my amazing breakthrough to the Surface, I realized, while still floundering in the Deep End, that God expected me to learn new ways to help myself push off from the Bottom. He wanted me to reach out and get the help I needed to begin my upward journey. I prayed that God would help me do this. He answered my request by sending me the people, the medical resources, the coping skills, and the self-care strategies I would need to begin my way back to the Top.

The first group of people He sent me was my healthcare team. I believe the most crucial parts of that team were my medical doctors, including both my primary care physicians and my rheumatologists. Because of the nature of my health issues, I depended on many types of doctors to help me manage my symptoms.

Joanne Zeis, has Behcet's, herself. In her latest book, Behcet's Disease, she explains that Behcet's is a rheumatic illness, causing inflammation and pain in numerous areas of the body, including the musculoskeletal system, which is composed of joints, bones, tendons, and muscles. For this reason, Zeis encourages people with Behcet's to see a rheumatologist as their main medical contact. However, she adds that, depending on what body sites are involved, it may also be necessary to meet with numerous other types of specialists, such as ophthalmologists, dermatologists, gastroenterologists, cardiologists, neurologists, and immunologists. According to Zeis, Behcet's causes vasculitis or inflammation of the blood vessels, and she adds that "wherever this inflammation shows up in the body is where the person experiences symptoms" (Zeis, 2015).

I am grateful for those doctors who helped me in the early days of my illness as well as for those on my treatment team today. When Dr. Lane decided to leave private practice, I hated to see her leave. I, then, was referred to Dr. Sydney Lawler, an outstanding clinician. She, like Dr. Lane, took the extra time needed to deal with my complex issues. She even organized all my records for me, without me asking her to do it. She also wrote a note to my clinical supervisor at Brookhaven explaining why I needed to set a limit on my work hours each week. Unfortunately, after only a few years, Dr. Lawler left private practice as well. Although Dr. Lawler was still my hospitalist, I was forced to find another outpatient primary care physician. I hoped and prayed that I would find one as competent and caring as Dr. Lane and Dr. Lawler had been.

I called Dr. Lane, told her my problem, and asked her for a referral. Among the list of physicians' names, she gave me was that of Dr. Dana Morrel. I promptly booked an appointment with her and have been her patient now for about nine years. Dr. Morrel is an extremely competent, kind, and compassionate internal medicine specialist. Once she wrote a note to my employer, explaining why I could not take a live-virus vaccine which was required for all hospital employees. She takes time explaining why something, such as a test or a new medicine is important. What I treasure about her is that she relates to me as one human being to another.

As mentioned earlier, three years after I first saw Dr. Morrel, my first rheumatologist stopped taking my insurance, prompting the need for me to find a new one. I am glad Dr. Morrel referred me to Dr. Debbie Gladd Foley, my current rheumatologist and treatment coordinator, who has made sure that I receive excellent care. Each time I see her I get a copy of her detailed Clinical Visit Summary on which she outlines my current medications, and my medical plan for the next three-month period. I value her thorough and organized approach to my healthcare, and I credit much of my improved daily functioning to her excellent clinical skills. She always takes time to address my issues of the day and never gives up on me. She is one of the most determined clinicians I have ever seen.

One of the first things that my doctors did for me was to give me a preliminary diagnosis of rheumatoid arthritis. Although the diagnosis has changed many times since I was first diagnosed in 1989, I found it much easier to manage daily symptoms after a name was attached to my problem. I often wondered why it is so important for people with chronic illness to have a name for what is happening to them.

Cheri Register suggests in her book, The Chronic Illness Experience: Embracing the Imperfect Life, that when the doctors give our illness a name, they help return some of our control over its place in our life. A diagnosis helps us remember that there is still a 'me' apart from confusing symptoms that have taken over our lives. She concludes, "The diagnosis gives you the perspective you need to revise your story" (Register, 1987).

As mentioned earlier, my one name turned into many names. Some names like MS and Wegener's were ruled out; Sjogren's syndrome and Raynaud's phenomenon were left on my list. Right after my diagnosis, I had a difficult time understanding why I was developing so many of these secondary conditions. In the years following, however, I learned this was not that unusual. It seems that in an autoimmune illness when your own system turns on you, it often starts a chain reaction.

Mary Shomon was diagnosed with an autoimmune disease called Hashimoto's thyroiditis. In her book, Living Well with Autoimmune Disease, she insists that after you develop an autoimmune process, you may begin a downward spiral which includes the development of other autoimmune issues. Multiple autoimmune illnesses are often complicated by "dramatically worsening allergies, heightened chemical sensitivities, hormonal imbalances, and a host of other debilitating and life-changing symptoms" (Shomon, 2002).

Two other authors, who have researched the patterns and effects of autoimmune disease are Baron-Faust and Buyon. Rita Baron-

Faust, an award-winning medical journalist and author of five books on women's health, has an autoimmune disease herself. She along with Jill Buyon, M.D., Professor of Medicine at the New York University School of Medicine, have co-authored a book entitled, The Autoimmune Connection: Essential Information for Women on Diagnosis, Treatment, and Getting on with Your Life (2002). In this book, the authors describe how attacks on your immune system have numerous targets. Thus, if you have one autoimmune disease, there's a good chance that you may develop a second or even a third disease. Autoimmune attacks (called flares) may occur in waves, with lulls in between. A person with autoimmune disease may then experience symptoms for weeks or months but then go into remission feeling perfectly fine. They also warn those with autoimmune disease to make certain their doctor treating them looks out for these additional diseases and are aware that they occur (Baron-Faust and Buyon, 2002).

As mentioned in Chapter One, my first overlap condition to arrive on the scene was Sjogren's syndrome. It occurs when a person's immune system attacks the eyes and mouth as though they were foreign bodies. A type of white blood cell (lymphocyte) targets and invades moisture-producing glands, such as the tear glands and the saliva glands, preventing them from producing moisture. (Fremes & Carterton, 2003). Moreover, Sjogren's can do more than produce dryness in the eyes and mouth. Since the dryness upsets the bio flora in the eyes, mouth, and throat, this disease provides opportunistic infections a perfect medium for rapid growth.

This can result in other secondary conditions such as eye infections, dental cavities, gum inflammation, oral thrush, and esophagitis, to name a few. The treatment for these problems includes daily use of topicals, such as moisturizing mouthwash, oral gel, throat spray, and lozenges for the mouth and throat. Regular dental appointments for cleaning and check-ups are an important part of managing Sjogren's in the mouth. For the eyes, regular use of moisture replacement tears or anti-inflammatory drops can be helpful.

My second overlap diagnosis was Raynaud's phenomenon. As mentioned in Chapter One, I was given Procardia, which helped me manage my Raynaud's. It's also important for me to avoid stress, dress warmly in cold weather, (wear heavy socks or layers of socks, wear gloves or mittens when it is cold), and use insulated containers to hold cold drinks.

This disorder can be seriously complicated by smoking, since smoking causes narrowing of blood vessels and increases attacks of Raynaud's. One of the worst cases of Raynaud's I ever witnessed occurred in a woman who refused to quit smoking. Even when she had one leg amputated, she continued to smoke. She eventually lost her other leg and only a few weeks later, she passed away.

As mentioned above, another characteristic of Behcet's disease is that it often requires a host of specialists to treat its typically wide-ranging symptoms. In the process of managing Behcet's and the overlap conditions resulting from it, I have relied on the care of numerous medical professionals. My gratitude goes to a host of other specialists who have provided me with care, such as neurologists, ENT's, ophthalmologists, gastroenterologists, gynecologists, urologists, dermatologists, nurses, laboratory technicians, and physical therapists. It seems that every time I got to the point I thought I couldn't go on, God would send me just the right doctor, nurse, therapist, or medication that would help me manage the problem facing me at that time.

But how do doctors arrive at a diagnosis? They first take a health history, which includes a family history of medical problems, personal symptoms, and earlier diagnoses. They also look for any clinical signs of illness in the body when they examine the patient. In addition, doctors have access to standard laboratory evaluations, such as sedimentation rate (ESR), which measures the amount of inflammation showing up in the blood at the time the test is done. They can also order a test called rheumatoid factor (RF), which can indicate whether a person has rheumatoid arthritis, and they can schedule another laboratory test designed to check for levels of antibodies in the blood, known as anti-nuclear antibodies (ANA/ANF), which can help diagnose such conditions as lupus, Sjogren's, or scleroderma, among others. These are just a sampling of diagnostic tests available to doctors treating autoimmune musculoskeletal disease (Kavanaugh, 2017) (Rodriguez, 2012) (Hua, 2017) (Vasconcelos, 2015; WebMD, Retrieved 2017).

However, the problem with all these blood tests is that there are a significant number of false positives and false negatives. For example, a person's test results may show a positive RF level, and she may not have rheumatoid disease or even be sick at all. In addition, she may have no symptoms and have a positive reading on this test. On the other hand, a person may have acute rheumatoid arthritis signs in the body (such as red, warm, swollen joints) and a history of other symptoms, such as morning stiffness, pain in joints even at rest, and extreme fatigue, and have a negative RF reading on this same test. The same is true for the ANA results. A person's test may reveal a positive ANA, and she may not have lupus or any other type of autoimmune disease. In contrast, a person may have a negative reading and be extremely ill (Kavanaugh, retrieved, 2017). This is especially true for Behcet's disease, which has no standardized blood test to identify it, although, for many Behcet's patients, certain of the above tests may produce positive results (Zeis, 2015).

This means that with these conditions, for some unfortunate patients, like me in the early days, who showed clear signs and reported significant symptoms; the doctors are forced to rely more on what they see and what they hear reported by the patient than by relying on lab tests alone. For almost thirty years now, my lab tests have shown very little about my disease activity that was made evident by signs in my body. This was extremely difficult for me during the first few years.

However, in more recent times my labs have picked up such things as a reduced T-cell immunity and chronic leukopenia (low white cell count). However, the following tests have always been normal: ESR, RF, and ANA, with one exception in 2012, when ANA was strongly positive (1080 when negative is less than 40). After years of living with frustrating symptoms yet with few consistently positive laboratory findings, I have come to believe that Behcet's is a hit-and-run disease, striking out of the shadows and then returning to the shadows when labs are ordered.

For this reason, I will always be grateful to my first rheumatologist, who as mentioned earlier, was able to give me that name even before getting any positive lab test results. Surprisingly, about 40% of early rheumatoid arthritis patients have negative lab results (Kavanaugh, retrieved 2017, Hua, et al., 2017). Unfortunately, for some of us who have complex health histories, an accurate diagnosis takes a long time to achieve. This is especially true if one has symptoms that are not always supported by the diagnostic tests or are not clearly visible at the time of the office visit; has symptoms in multiple body systems; has a rare disorder; have several overlap diseases; or has a shifting pattern of symptoms which move from one body system to another.

That is why it was important, especially in the beginning, for me to do my homework and try to find doctors who looked at more than standardized laboratory tests – ones who also considered clinical signs in the body and were willing to look at pictures of those signs (as suggested by the American Behcet's Disease Association) when they occurred at random and were not always visible on the day of my appointment (Zeis, 2003).

I also learned that autoimmune disease can often run in families. Both rheumatoid arthritis and Behcet's disease and many other autoimmune conditions can have family connections. However, according to Baron-Faust and Buyon, family members won't always have the same type of illness. According to them, one family may have immune cells which attack the thyroid, while another member may have cells that attack the joints. They also point out that even if you are an identical twin, your chances of having the same kind of illness may vary (Baron-Faust and Buyon, 2002).

Nevertheless, family patterns can reflect a strong genetic predisposition to autoimmune arthritis. As I mentioned earlier, in my family, my sister had some form of rheumatoid disease that was never accurately diagnosed. I have two aunts who had rheumatoid arthritis, with hand deformities. The authors also insist, however, that just because I might inherit the same abnormal gene as another family member, it usually takes something else in the environment, such as stress or a virus to trigger that gene (Baron-Faust and Buyon, 2002).

Identifying the Enemy

One of the first things I needed to understand after my diagnosis was that the main source of my autoimmune disease process was inflammation. Whether it was RA, Sjogren's, Raynaud's or Behcet's, it all came down to the same core issue: inflammation. Over the years, I learned that the same immune system (comprised of white blood cells) which was designed to fight off threats from the outside world, such as bacteria, viruses, and even cancer; can, in turn, create debilitating and life-threatening syndromes (Baron-Faust & Buyon, 2002).

I also discovered that, while my immune system was busy attacking its own tissue, it could no longer do a good job of attacking outside invaders. I battled various types of infections. These infections included opportunistic infections which are caused by microbes which normally co-exist with humans (on skin or in mouth or throat, for example) but which, in the immune-compromised patient, outgrow their normal population size and wreak havoc (Vasconcelos, 2015).

Thus, when my inflammation went unchecked for very long, I not only experienced a Behcet's flare, I was also more prone to get some type of infection, even when I was not taking an immunosuppressant medication. The irony of the Behcet's autoimmune reaction is that it can produce an increase of one kind of immune cell, thus causing an inflammatory response, which can attack body tissues; while at the same time, reducing the number of another type of immune cell, thus causing a suppressed immune response, which can allow for increased opportunistic and other regular types of infections (Kahan, 1992) (Lim, 1983).

My most frequent Behcet's symptoms now are joint and cartilage pain, mouth and skin lesions, and eye inflammation. As mentioned in

Chapter Three, it is not unusual for people who have Behcet's and who go untreated, to develop blindness due to the inflammation in the eyes. Fortunately, I have had only mild inflammation in the eyes, (episcleritis or inflammation of the outside of the eye). This may be because I received aggressive treatment early from excellent doctors.

As a person with Behcet's disease, I learned not to ignore an important fact when I was deciding on what type of treatment was best for me. My research has shown that Behcet's disease can, at times, also affect the heart, the lungs, the liver, the intestines, the brain and central nervous system, and other organs in the body as well. However, these complications are much less frequent than problems in the skin and eyes (Dunkin, Retrieved, 2017) (Zeis, 2015).

Battle Plans

Another tool I used to push off from the Bottom of the Pool was a treatment plan. After the diagnosis, the next step was to decide on how to reduce the inflammation and to modify my pain level. This is usually done with a trial-and-error approach. Unfortunately, with autoimmune disease, there often is no "one-size-fits-all" method of turning off the renegade process that is causing us so many problems in our bodies. There are, however, standard treatment protocols, that can guide the doctors in their treatment decisions.

One of the first types of treatment my doctors gave me for managing my chronic inflammatory arthritis was medications to reduce the inflammation in the joints. The first tier of drugs commonly used for inflammation are medications called non-steroidal anti-inflammatories (NSAIDS), such as Voltaren and Naprosyn. When these types of drugs didn't work, I was given Prednisone, (an oral steroid), Ridaura (oral gold), Plaquenil, and Methotrexate. Prednisone worked for a while but caused severe stomach pain when taken on a long-term basis. As mentioned earlier, Methotrexate worked well, but I had to go off this drug due to side-effects in the muscles.

Later I benefited from the anti-tumor-necrosis-factor drugs, Enbrel and Humira. These worked for me initially, but the Enbrel caused side-effects that I couldn't tolerate, and I had to go off it as well. Humira worked well at first and helped me more consistently than any others that I have had. However, it began to be less effective and its cost became prohibitive. That is why Dr. Gladd Foley decided to put me on Remicade therapy. This drug has reduced the number of my flares, decreased my pain significantly, and dramatically improved my daily functioning. All these improvements translate into one important benefit: a higher quality of life.

After I was given a treatment plan by my doctor, it was my responsibility to work that plan. It was important for me to take the medication just as it was prescribed in the amounts and the frequency that the doctor discussed in the appointment. If I later had problems with side-effects, I agreed to contact the doctor who prescribed the medication. It was then my doctor's responsibility to help me manage these negative consequences from treatment.

If I had been fortunate enough to have found relief of painful symptoms, I might have decided the side-effects were not serious enough for me to stop taking the medication. For example, some more minor symptoms, such as nausea, diarrhea, benign rashes, or increased number of infections may be worth tolerating to achieve a relief from the inflammation. One example is the reaction I developed after taking the oral gold. I developed a rash over my entire body, from the scalp to the bottoms of my feet. I was diagnosed with pseudo-folliculitis and given a topical medication to apply daily. After using the topical for about a week, the rash cleared, and I was able to stay on this medicine until my doctor decided it was not an effective treatment for me.

On the other hand, there are some side-effects that cannot be tolerated. A good example of this is my visual deficits resulting from Plaquenil treatment. This drug's major side-effect, retinal toxicity, can cause retinal atrophy and holes in the visual field, which, if left unchecked, can result in blindness. Unfortunately, even after this drug is discontinued, the retinal atrophy can continue indefinitely. There is no medical algorithm that can tell how much damage will be done by measuring either the person's drug dosage or length of treatment (Hansen, Mark S., M.D. and Stefanie G. Schuman, M.D. , 2011). It is an uncharted area for the patient's ophthalmologist.

Another potential side-effect of arthritis treatment is infection. This is especially true for those who take the biologic medications, such as Enbrel, Humira, or Remicade (anti-TNF drugs). As mentioned earlier, TNF stands for tumor necrosis factor, which is an inflammatory molecule that often causes organ and tissue damage. This molecule is overactive in some types of autoimmune disease. Enbrel, Humira, and Remicade all suppress TNF, but they do it in different ways. Enbrel and Humira soak up the TNF like a sponge, rendering it inactive. Remicade, in contrast, uses a smart bomb molecule called a monoclonal antibody to deactivate TNF (Baron-Faust & Buyon, 2002). For most of the time during my treatment with these drugs, this has meant an increase in sinus and urinary tract infections. Of course, my problem then became finding out which antibiotic would kill a particular microbe. For years, fighting recurrent infections has become a regular part of my life. Nevertheless, I personally believe that the improved quality of life that I experience from taking the immunosuppressant medications is worth the risk.

Other potential side-effects of TNF-inhibitors include a reactivation of hepatitis B and/or tuberculosis and certain types of allergic reactions. Less common reactions are neurological disorders, cardiac issues, and a lupus-like syndrome (Ruffing, 2016). These are much less likely than infection, but they must be considered when deciding whether to take the biologic or not. This is the reason regular blood tests are required when taking these high-risk medications. Ultimately, when I have tried different medications in my treatment, it has meant that I have needed to work with my doctors to weigh the benefits of the medication against the risks of taking the drug.

Another issue that my doctors are responsible for helping me manage is pain, which is one of the major symptoms of rheumatological disease. This is the symptom that was the most difficult for me to cope with during the first few years after my first onset. There were two main types of pain which I had the most difficulty with during this time. The first was from the joints, such as elbows, knees, feet, and hands. The hands were the hardest to deal with, because I needed my hands for so many of my activities of daily living. Another type of pain I dealt with was muscle pain. This appeared in the form of an aching neck and back or in the form of the all-over flu-like aching, known as myalgia. There have been times when the aching was so bad I had to take three hot showers per day just to keep going. Obviously, this was before the medications began to turn the disease around for me.

One of the first things that my doctor did was to prescribe pain medication. I found that regular dosing with milder, non-addictive pain medications worked well for me. In other words, if I waited until I began to hurt to take the pain medicine, the milder drug would do nothing. I would then need a stronger pain medication to modify my pain at all. However, I soon learned that if I kept the milder pain medication in my system, it worked beautifully without causing withdrawal or compromising my mental clarity.

One of the biggest problems in our society today is the abuse of pain medications, especially opioids. For many years, large numbers of people who have chronic pain have been taking certain kinds of opioids, for example, oxycodone (OxyContin), or hydrocodone plus acetaminophen (Vicodin/Lortab). Unfortunately, although these are highly effective in relieving intractable pain, they carry with them a very real risk of addiction and even death from abuse and overdosing (Nat. Inst. On Drug Abuse, retrieved 8/26/17; Maryland Addiction Recovery Center, 2014). Also, they can rid the body of its own natural painkillers called endorphins (Brown, et al, 2006), decrease mental clarity, and increase the risk of depression and degenerative changes in an aging brain (Brown, et al, 2006; Barg, et al., 1993). People who have severe pain should not feel guilty about taking these types of medications, however, the long-term side-effects must be taken into consideration when deciding which pain medication is necessary.

Not Just Pills but Coping Skills

Another resource I used to receive information on pain management was the Arthritis Foundation. From their seminars and management classes, I gained helpful information about non-drug pain management strategies as well as pain management tools. I learned how to perform tasks in a way that would not put as much strain on my joints. I invested in lighter weight cooking utensils and dishes, and in a jar- opener mounted under the top cabinets. I even found a mitt that could be warmed in the microwave. It stayed warm for about twenty minutes and helped decrease the aching and soreness in my hands. In addition, I learned that heating pads can often relieve the discomfort in my chest wall, neck, back, arms, shoulders, and hands. They are strategically placed in my home so that whenever I have a rest break, I can also heat and relax tight muscles. However, it's important to be careful not to use them on areas that lack good circulation or on desensitized skin. Doing so can cause severe burns on these desensitized areas.

Another common symptom of chronic illness I have had to deal with is fatigue. I found that my endurance and stamina and ability to function well depended not only on how well the medications were working, but also on my ability to listen to my body. I learned it was crucial to give my body the amount of rest it needed balanced with the right amount of exercise on a regular basis.

The Gel

With arthritis, the morning's an adventure for me,
To learn what the pain of that first move will be,
And which part of my body will be the most sore,
As my head laves the pillow and my feet touch the floor.

Will it now be a leg, a hip, or an arm?
Or a foot or an ankle to give first alarm?
Will a shoulder, an elbow, a knee first complain?

Deborah K Steen

Or will hands be the sorest and give the most pain?

Will I feel like a puppet that lost all its strings?
Or more like a silly goose minus its wings?
Like the Tin Man before Dorothy oiled him down?
Or a wooden toy soldier marching to town?

Will I shift to the left or shift to the right?
Which side is stiffer now after last night?
Will I hobble to breakfast or walk in with ease?
Will my fingers be working or will they just freeze?

Is it sunny or rainy? . . . are there clouds in the sky?
Is it colder or wetter? . . . is a front moving by?
The weather's a player in this game, you see,
It can even decide just how stiff I will be.

After breakfast and pill's, a hot shower's the thing
That can really do wonders . . . what relief it can bring.
And later a PACE tape can really do well
To oil all the "hinges" and vanquish "THE GEL."

(Deborah Steen, 1989)

The Myth of Superwoman

It seems ironic to me that while I was plunging toward the
Bottom of the Pool, I was learning some important lessons about

90

myself and about life in general. I had developed a false sense of security about that inner tube when I was six-years-old. As an adult, I came to embrace a different illusion that let me down just as certainly as the kid's inflatable of my youth. This was the false paradigm that I describe as the Myth of Superwoman.

My illness put the brakes on my energy, and I suddenly realized that I had run out of the ability to push myself as I used to. I tried to compensate for lack of energy by continuing to keep an unrealistic schedule for my day. I had a weekly list and a monthly list. The problem with the lists was that I sometimes let the list control me instead of me controlling the list. Even worse, if I didn't accomplish everything I put on the list that morning, I considered myself a failure for that day.

As a matter of fact, I came to understand that refusing to acknowledge my true limitations and trying to push beyond them to reach some arbitrary standard of excellence could compromise my own physical, emotional, and spiritual health.

Therefore, I learned to divide my work into smaller units and replaced work-based pacing with time-based. Time-based pacing is an adaptive approach that has often been helpful when I am in a flare. Depending on what is reasonable to accommodate my limited energy, which varies from day to day, I might decide to work for one hour or thirty minutes on a task before resting rather than working to complete the task. I could then monitor the amount I was able to accomplish within the time-frame to create a more realistic expectation of how many days a project would take, or if it was even worth the amount of time required. If it was a necessity, I could always recruit and delegate. My daughters received assignments to help around the house. As a result, my time and energy spread further, and they had the opportunity to practice basic life-skills.

Some people who have significant chronic illness and pain may be able to continue with their old habits and accomplish amazing things despite their health issues. I know that God can use these special people to inspire others to avoid 'giving in' to their illness and pain and becoming less active than they could be. However, I also believe, at times, God may have a plan for the tortoises among us, or those people God decides to slow down so they can recognize the new purpose He has for them. I submit that these "slowed-down people" can perhaps do as much or more to achieve God's purpose in their lives in their new, unhurried pace than they could in their former breakneck lunge toward the finish line.

Another harsh reality set in during my time in Deep Water. I learned perfection in any aspect of my life was not a realistic goal for me. I always loved to have a clean house and to cook elaborate meals for family and friends. After the Big Plunge, it was a challenge just to make sure everyone was fed three times a day. Housecleaning changed dramatically as well. I also came to accept that my house did not need to be cleaned from top to bottom every week. I learned to get a bit more comfortable with dusty furniture, and I also learned to tolerate clutter in the bedrooms. When I cleaned, I didn't cook. We would have some sort of pre-made meal or take-out. When I cooked, I didn't clean anything but the dishes.

I also learned to manage the fatigue by accepting the fact that planning ahead was a must for me. I needed to manage my life in such a way as to get the most out of the heart of each day. My schedule has changed dramatically over the years. Each day still begins with self-care, which I consider primary in managing my illness. Gone is the time when the unfinished items on my list bully me into thinking I have failed. Instead, I now review the fact that my body, which I have learned to love and respect all over again, has carried me through another day.

FINDING UP AGAIN

Chronic Illness and Depression

After I achieved success in establishing a professional healthcare team to help me identify a firm diagnosis and to create a treatment plan, I then was responsible for following up with that plan. This included learning new ways to manage pain and fatigue and creating new habits of self-care. However, one of the most important steps I took to take care of myself came later, when I encountered depression.

As mentioned earlier, after I experienced the first Wegener's scare in 1994, I developed depression symptoms that did not go away. Some of these symptoms were a feeling of hopelessness about my future, an inability to stay asleep, difficulty concentrating, memory difficulties, and chronic irritability. I was fortunate that Dr. Lane picked up on these symptoms and encouraged me to get the professional help I needed. I also realized from my training in psychology how important it was to address these issues if I wanted to feel better.

It is not unusual for people who have chronic medical conditions to become depressed. In fact, it's estimated that up to one-third of people challenged by a serious medical issue experience some type of clinical depression. Serious illness causes significant changes in a person's lifestyle, often decreasing one's mobility and independence. In addition, a disease or chronic pain condition that doesn't go away with treatment may make it impossible to pursue the activities that person enjoyed before the onset of the illness. Chronic illness can ultimately "undermine self-confidence and a sense of hope in the future." It is, thus, understandable that "people with chronic illness often experience a certain amount of despair and sadness" (WebMD online site, 2017).

Carol Sveilich, in her book, Just Fine: Unmasking Concealed Chronic Illness and Pain, insists that it is not hard to understand why people with significant types of chronic illness are often depressed. She asks, "Who wouldn't be depressed if they were dealing with such persistent and debilitating symptoms?" (Sveilich, 2005) However, depression specialist, Dr. Arthur Rifkin gives another viewpoint on depression. He insists that although depression is an understandable reaction to chronic illness, it is important that depression symptoms should be distinguished from the symptoms of the physical disorder itself and treated appropriately (Sveilich, 2005) (National Institute of Mental Health (NIMH), 2016).

I believe that both ideas are valid. Depression is understandable in significant types of chronic illness. Nevertheless, just because it is understandable, this does not mean that it should not be considered a serious complication of the illness and, thus, properly diagnosed and treated as a separate issue in and of itself.

Dr. Genee Jackson identifies depression as "the most common associated symptom of chronic pain and illness." Dr. Jackson also points out that when a person experiences pain or illness that is ongoing, that person uses an enormous amount of energy in just living from moment to moment, and often loses the true joy of living in the emotional fog that often accompanies intractable pain.

She explains how depression affects the body. It can alter the biochemistry in such a way as to induce sleep deprivation, thereby lowering serotonin levels, which can aggravate the original medical problem. Dr. Jackson further concludes that, in the case of these physical depression symptoms, such as changes in appetite (eating more than usual/eating less than usual) or sleep difficulties, the person often responds well to antidepressant medication (Sveilich, 2005).

One of the first steps I took to treat my depression was to take an anti-depressant, which made a big difference in my sleep patterns, in my mood, and in my overall functioning daily. However, at the same time, I also saw a counselor to help me process my grief issues surrounding the illness.

Dealing with Loss

Elizabeth Kubler-Ross, a psychiatrist who was one of the foremost authorities on the psychology of grief, included depression as one of the five stages of grief: denial, anger, bargaining, depression, acceptance. (Kubler-Ross, 1969)

It's easy to understand that grief is a normal consequence of one's mourning the death of a loved one. What's not always understood, however, is that, when a person develops a chronic illness; she is mourning the death of her healthy self, of the person she once was. This, too, requires the same grief process that Ross outlined in her book.

However, it is also important to distinguish depression as the fourth stage of the grief process from clinical depression that includes symptoms that last more than two weeks and cause a significant amount of dysfunction, complicating the healing process and even making the medical problem itself more severe. If a person has sadness or hopelessness and any of these other symptoms listed that last at least two weeks or more, he should realize that this is a serious health complication that needs to be addressed by his doctor or mental health professional.

Symptoms of Depression

- Persistent sad, anxious, or "empty" mood
- Feelings of hopelessness, or pessimism
- Irritability
- Feelings of guilt, worthlessness, or helplessness
- Loss of interest or pleasure in hobbies and activities
- Decreased energy or fatigue
- Moving or talking more slowly

- Felling restless or having trouble sitting still
- Difficulty concentrating, remembering, or making decisions
- Difficulty sleeping, early-morning awakening, or oversleeping
- Aches or pains, headaches, cramps, or digestive problems without a clear physical cause and/or that do not ease with treatment
(NIMH, Rev., 2016)

For the person with a chronic illness, the grief issue centers around the losses that the person has experienced due to the chronic health condition. In my own case, I experienced the following losses: loss of mobility, loss of energy and vitality, loss of enjoyment of activities I once found fulfilling and now were only a trigger for more pain, loss of perceived identity (being a good wife to my husband and a good mother to my two daughters), loss of predictability in my life due to the inability to achieve an accurate diagnosis, (or, at other times, from having too many diagnoses), loss of dreams of what I wanted to accomplish in my life, and, last of all, and most importantly, a loss of hope that things were going to get better.

Clearly, I was not the only person who experienced losses due to this unwelcome guest. It is important for family members as well to recognize and grieve their own losses from the illness of their family member. Children, especially, need to be encouraged to talk about their feelings and have them validated. When a mom has a chronic illness, this can often give the child the message, "There is something wrong with my family." The most difficult conclusion that the child can read from this message is, "There is something wrong with me."

As I learned through my therapy and through my study of psychology, if I ever wanted to make my way Up again, I had to grieve these losses and find, with God's help, a way to redefine my own identity and reset my life goals according to the limitations that were now a part of my new reality. As I made progress toward acceptance, it made it easier for others in my family to achieve a new normal.

An important first step was for me to refocus not on what I had lost, but what I had left. I learned that I needed to redefine success for myself. At the Bottom of the Pool, I found it easy to compare myself to healthy people. When I did this, I focused on my losses and saw myself as a failure. When I began to find Up again, I came to recognize all the energy, skills, and talents I still had left. I then was able to create a new definition of success for myself that would allow me to accomplish new life goals by my learning how to adapt to my own new limitations.

A Mother with RA

I'm a mother of two with RA,
And every morning I pray
For the strength just to be
The mom I should be,
And to make it through one more day.
There's the laundry, the cooking, the beds;
The washing and drying of heads;
There's the car-pooling, too,
And the shopping to do,

And the storybooks still to be read.
There's the housecleaning done in three parts;
That's done with its stops and its starts;
There's the laundry to fold,
While nursing a cold,
Or tending a skinned knee that smarts.
There's the kissing away of the hurts;
And the pressing of blouses and skirts;
And the schoolwork, too
Each day to review,
With their Reeboks all covered with dirt.
But this is the time I adore,
It' the time when they walk through the door,
My heart gets a tug,
As I feel a soft hug,
And hear, "Mom, I sure love you!" once more.

(Deborah Steen, 1990)

A Model of Transitions

Bruce McIntyre is currently the Director of the Parkinson Foundation of Oklahoma. In his book, Graceful Transitions: An Inspirational Guide for Family Caregivers and Care Receivers, Bruce proposes that another way to look at chronic illness is to see it as a series of transitions. He describes this adaptive process in dealing with a chronic illness and about how all such transitions involve three distinct phases, quoting from William Bridges' Model of Transitions.

According to the Bridges model, anytime we experience significant change in our lives, we are faced with the fact that something has ended. Usually, our first reaction is denial, and we try to believe that nothing is different. We try to hold onto this denial, but, as Bridges explains, "Somewhere behind our eyes, we know the truth that something has ended."

After accepting that something has ended, we enter a "neutral zone," a place where "life is all questions and no answers." In this transition stage, we are uncertain about what we should do next. This is a time of grieving what has changed. The length of one's stay in the neutral zone will depend on our ability and determination to learn and explore new options and grow to the next transition.

In the last stage of the transition, after we have accepted our new reality, we come to accept and even embrace our "new beginning." However, we should not expect that in this stage everything will return to normal. It probably won't. However, what it does mean is that we are attempting to adapt and are trying out new solutions and are "experimenting with a new normal" (McIntyre, 2012).

Never Give Up

Donoghue and Siegel are two clinical psychologists, who have worked for many years with numerous people who have chronic illness. In their book, Sick and Tired of Feeling Sick and Tired: Living with Invisible Chronic Illness, they explain their ideas about what they have learned by working with these individuals. They insist that none of these people permanently arrived at some destination labeled 'acceptance.' Instead, what these two psychologists witnessed was an "ongoing, ever-changing process" continuing through the years and requiring, from the people themselves, an amazing amount of patience and courage. According to Donoghue and Siegel:

> These individuals are constantly learning about their bodies, their needs, their limits, and capabilities. They don't deny their illness; they haven't given up or given in. They accept what life has given them with dignity and peace. (Donoghue & Siegel, 2000).

Donoghue and Siegel explain that a person with chronic illness often encounters problems on the road to achieving acceptance. Whereas they insist that acceptance is essential to successfully living with chronic illness, they quickly add that true acceptance does not mean giving in or giving up. They encourage their readers and audiences to stretch themselves to never stop growing. Nevertheless, they point out how important it is for those with chronic illness to know their own true limits that are imposed by their illness. They insist that pushing beyond those limits fosters "powerlessness and self-defeat." They remind people who are "sick and tired of being sick and tired" that a "genuine 'no' forms a foundation for the process of discovering and accepting realistic limits" (Donaghue & Siegel, 2000).

These two psychologists give a living example of this adaptive reaction by sharing the story of Leon Fleisher, a renowned concert pianist, who was diagnosed with carpal tunnel syndrome. They explain how he didn't give up but accepted the unfortunate fact that he had a chronic pain condition and, thus, could no longer play the piano with his right hand. Fleisher, instead, accepted his own new reality and had concertos written for the left hand, thereby, continuing his music career courageously and without self-pity.

Fleisher thus avoided two non-adaptive options after discovering he had carpel tunnel syndrome. He could have remained in denial and tried unsuccessfully to play with his right hand, which, when he failed, would set him up for depression. On the other extreme, he could have just given up playing the piano altogether, bemoaning his fate, which, like the first option, could have invited a feeling of damaged goods and its companion feeling – depression. As these two authors point out, "Admitting the truth has nothing to do with giving up. To the contrary, creativity can thrive within the boundaries of accepted limits" (Donoghue & Siegel, 2000).

Another good example of this idea is found in the life of Chester Carlson. As a young engineer, Carlson worked as a patent analyzer for an electrical component maker. His job included making multiple copies of drawings and documents that were to be submitted to the patent office to register his company's inventions and ideas. Redrawing the copies took hours. Moreover, Carlson was nearsighted and had a severe form of inflammatory arthritis in his hands which was making it increasingly difficult for him to continue to do his job. He knew that because of his worsening arthritis, he would not be able to continue making these laborious hand copies indefinitely.

Then he thought to himself that there had to be a better way to do this job. He used his engineering skills and went to work in his home to find an alternative to hand-copying the patent drawings. He had an idea for a reproduction technique called electrophotography. He filed for a patent for this process in 1937. However, when he approached companies like IBM, GE, and RCA, he was turned away. It took him another twenty years to at last find a business interested in his new technology. After years of rejection, he, at last, took his ideas to the Haloid Company, which later changed its name to Xerox. This company finally brought Carlson's copying technology to market in 1960 (Lemelson-MIT Program, Retrieved 2017).

Carlson, then, had progressed to the final stage of the Bridges Model of Transitions. He had accepted the reality of his new normal and found a way to adapt and to use his talents in a way that accommodated his own unique personal limitations and held out even in the face of years of professional rejection. Not only did Carlson help himself by finding a creative way to do his job, but, in addition, because he didn't give up, he made the job of making copies much less tedious for all of us.

Unexpected Gifts

My ascent from the Bottom of the Pool was much easier when I realized the illness had not only brought losses into my life but gifts as well. One of the gifts that my illness gave me was the importance of reassessing my priorities. I was forced to slow down and look very closely at my values and my life goals and make sure that my daily routines and patterns of behavior were in line with these values and goals. Because of my limited energy and stamina, I had no time to waste on activities that I had once thought were important, but now realized were not productive or contributing to better health, relaxation, or spiritual growth.

One example of this change of viewpoint came when I started back to school. The illness had taught me the importance of self-care. During my undergraduate degree program, I had considered anything less than an A, a failure on my part. I pushed myself to make good grades and averaged only four hours of sleep per night. However, when I returned to school working with a chronic illness to manage, I told myself that if I could get an A that was great, but if I had to push myself to the point of risking my health to get that A, it wasn't worth it. I gave myself permission to make a B and still take care of myself. I never regretted that decision.

Another gift the illness gave me was the gift of a heightened sensitivity to others in pain, both physical and emotional. This became clear when I later worked as both an inpatient and outpatient therapist. One lady, after seeing me for only one session, said, "You are so easy to talk to, I feel that I have known you for a long time. I have never told anyone the things that I have told you." I believe that this compassion and concern for my patients was a gift from God that my own struggles had brought into my life. They made me a better counselor, and, with God at my side, they helped turn something negative in my own life into something positive in someone else's life.

A Case for Support

Another thing that helped me begin to find Up again was the tremendous support systems in my own life. These supports were other gifts from the illness. The first support system that helped me find my way again was my amazing family. My husband, Bill, was a tremendous source of strength through the darkest of times. He was the one who encouraged me the most to go back to school and get my master's degree. He believed in me and provided me with a sounding board for the many frustrations of having a difficult-to-diagnose medical condition.

Next, there were my two daughters, Jennifer and Amanda, who gave me two more very good reasons not to give up. At a young age of four and five, they learned to do things around the house to help. Moreover, their extra-curricular activities kept me going to get them to all the places that they needed to be during the day, such as piano, or band, or play practice. I believe that if it had not been for them keeping me busy, I would have had more opportunity to isolate and become even more depressed. I tried to sandwich in their activities with my evening graduate courses and library time. One of the main reasons I went back to school to get my master's degree was to model an example to my girls, showing them that I refused to remain a victim of the illness, and that one can find a way to take a negative experience and turn it into a positive outcome for that person and for the people she encounters along the way. I consider Bill and the girls my three best motivations for me to get better.

Another gift has been my church family. From the time I was first diagnosed with RA in 1989, one of my best cheerleaders and spiritual mentors was Marvin Phillips. In Chapter Four, I explained how important his phone call was at a turning point in my life. Marvin's positive Christian example gave me a tremendous amount of strength right after I became ill. Marvin had been on the same rosters as Robert Schuller and Zig Zigler, two nationally-known motivational speakers, who believed wholeheartedly in the power of positive Christian thinking in our lives.

Marvin had a Wednesday night class, entitled Peak of the Week, that was televised in the Tulsa area for many years. This class helped me learn a host of positive living skills. He told us that each person has two lists he carries around with him in his mental pocket. He said that in one pocket, he carries a list of all the things wrong in his life: The Bad List. In the other pocket, he carries a list of all the things right in his life: The Good List. Marvin suggested every time someone asks him how he is doing, he can choose which of these two lists he wants to report from and which one stays in his pocket. Marvin always reminded us that everyone has a choice about which list comes out of the pocket.

I have used this example many times in both my depression

management groups and various support groups I have worked with in the Tulsa community. I have found that there are close friends and relatives and health professionals, who, when they ask us how we are doing, really want us to report from both lists. However, most people who ask how we are doing, are doing so mostly as a greeting, not as a solicitation of all our current health concerns. This is a good time to pick from the "Good List" and say "Great, thank you," or to just say "Hello, how are you?"

What I Think, I Am

Another way I found Up again was to change the way I thought about myself. Learning this process and using it in my own life and teaching it to my patients as well have been another gift the illness has brought me. The illness and the depression brought a whole list of negative thoughts about myself and about what my chances were to succeed now that I had a chronic illness holding me back. This kind of thinking was self-destructive and not helpful in my healing process. Most of these negative messages I am referring to were troublesome during the early years. Later, in my psychological studies, I came to learn just how these thoughts were self-defeating, and I learned how to reverse them and turn them into positive affirmations.

Cognitive Restructuring

1A Because of this illness, my life will never be the same.

1B My life may never be the same, but if I learn how to adapt, it might become, in some ways, even better.

2A I will have to take medicine for the rest of my life.

2B I'm so grateful I have medications that can make me better.

3A I'm not worth much to anyone anymore.

3B What I can learn about and share about from my illness is worth a lot to others who are struggling.

4A Today I am hurting so much I don't want to get out of bed.

4B Today I am hurting, but I know that after I get up, eat breakfast, take my medications, take a hot shower, and exercise, I will feel much better.

5A I think that no one understands how bad I feel.

5B I am blessed to have family and friends and doctors who try to understand what I am going through. They may not understand everything, but neither do I understand everything about people with other types of problems. I am grateful for their efforts at understanding.

This is called cognitive restructuring. Basically, it means changing my thinking from negative to positive. It all goes back to those two lists that Marvin was talking about. The A statements come from The Bad List. The B statements come from The Good List. I always have a choice of which one I am going to think about and focus on and report from daily. What I also learned in my studies is that the negative thoughts not only make me a difficult person to be around, they also increase my pain and prevent my body from healing.

Lori Hartwell, in her book, Chronically Happy: Joyful Living in Spite of Chronic Illness, explains the importance of reversing negative self-talk. She reveals that in the early stages of her own battle with chronic kidney disease, she felt as if she were broken and as if she were damaged goods. She shares how she learned to keep those thoughts away. She explains that as we learn to live with our illness, we discover that our minds can be our best friend, helping us stay in charge of our health management and enhancing our healing process (Hartwell, 2002).

However, Hartwell also says that our minds can do the opposite if not brought under control. She explains that our minds can become our worst enemy, keeping us locked into a victim mentality, thus, reinforcing the thought that we aren't good enough, healthy enough, or worthy enough to enjoy a successful life.

So how do we turn this negative thought pattern around so that we can heal our lives? Hartwell concludes that to take control of our runaway minds, we must reject negative, self-defeating messages about ourselves and our future, which only sabotage our chances of successfully managing our illness. We then need to replace these negative thoughts with positive, self-affirming messages, which enhance the healing process. This takes much practice and determination on our part.

Hartwell also admits that there are times when, despite all our attempts to reverse negative thinking, our minds still allow the negative thoughts to flourish. When this happens, the author has some great advice: "Take your body somewhere positive, and your mind will follow" (Hartwell, 2002). This may mean calling a friend for lunch, taking in a movie, going for a walk, attending a support group, or just reading a good book.

Hope is Real, and It Can Heal.

In addition to grieving losses and redefining success, for me to find Up again, I also needed to find ways to get my hope back. Dr. Bernie Siegel in his book, Love, Medicine, and Miracles, describes how important this hope really is. After spending years working with people with terminal cancer, he concluded that hope is one of the most important factors in the healing process.

> Hope is not statistical. It is physiological. The concepts of false hope and detached concern need to be discarded from the medical vocabulary. They are destructive for doctor and patient... All hope is real in a patient's mind (Siegel, 1986).

Dr. Siegel witnessed some exceptional people who had been diagnosed with end-stage cancer find their way back to health again when they held on to hope. He also witnessed something else that hope did for these people.

> Even if what you most hope for – a complete cure – doesn't come to pass, the hope itself can sustain you to accomplish many things in the meantime. Refusal to hope is nothing more

than a decision to die (Siegal, 1986).

Even medical researchers have proven that hope is a powerful drug. New drugs today are tested by a double-blind method. By this method of testing, the participating doctors, themselves, have no idea which of the drugs they are administering are the true drugs and which are the controls. The reason drugs must be tested this way is due to the power of human hope.

Philip Yancey, a well-known author, and theologian has written a book entitled, Where is God When It Hurts? In this book, Yancey explains that before medical scientists utilized double-blind studies, an unexpected result occurred in the research. Amazingly, almost all new drugs showed significantly positive results, regardless of their chemical content. Ultimately, the researchers discovered that a key factor in the drug's success was the demeanor of the doctor who administered it. Yancey points out that the doctor who participated in the study could, by his words, his voice, his attitude or his tone, unknowingly convey optimism and hope, thereby alerting the patient to the probability of their improvement (Yancey, 1990).

Yancey also describes pastor and author Bruce Larson's visit to the Menninger Clinic, where he asked the staff to tell him, in their opinions, what was the most important ingredient in treating severe mental illness. They all were unanimous in listing hope as the most important factor.

They said they could always tell right away when one of their patients achieved a renewed hope during their treatment – when they first believed that the future would not be as bad as the present. However, they went on to admit that they had no idea how to "dispense" hope to their patients. According to these experts in mental health treatment, hope is "an elusive gift" and is not something that can be taught, but it can, on occasion, be "caught." (Yancey, 1990) From my own personal experience of working more than fifteen years in mental health counseling, my colleagues and I continually searched for ways to awaken this courage to hope.

More than twenty years ago I began the work of getting my own hope back. One gift I treasure dearly is a silver pin with the word "hope" on it. A friend at church, Sharon Duffer, gave it to me two years ago after I had my surgery for what the doctors thought at first was cancer. As she pinned it on me, she told me, "Now you are a survivor!" When Sharon pinned that hope pin on me, I felt like a survivor. Not only had I survived an MS diagnosis, a Wegener's diagnosis, cellulitis surgery, a cancer diagnosis, and thirty years of living with an autoimmune disease; I had also survived clinical depression, the loss of hope. I was thankful to God that years before Sharon gave me this pin, I had succeeded in finding Up again, and by doing so, I had also recovered something precious I had lost--my hope. Now I was ready at last to continue my journey back to the Surface.

SWIM STROKES

It didn't take me long to realize that if I was ever going to make it off the Bottom of the Pool, I would have to learn how to Swim. The first Swim Strokes came when, as mentioned in Chapter Six, I chose a supportive healthcare team. However, although good healthcare is primary and vital to good disease management, this alone was not enough to get me off the Bottom. In time, I learned that reaching out for community support and reshaping personal long-term lifegoals which accommodated my own unique limitations were also important in helping me make it to the Top once again. For me this meant reconnecting to the community in three ways: (1) participating in community support groups to help me with my own health issues (2) getting the education I needed to accomplish modified life objectives and (3) using the skills I had learned in my own groups and in my professional life to help others at my work and in the community-at-large.

As mentioned in Chapter One, my first rheumatologist diagnosed me originally with rheumatoid arthritis and told me it was important for me to get in touch with the Arthritis Foundation to find information about my illness and to find support. She told me my family and friends would not always be able to understand what I was going through and that a support group would be a great asset in fighting the disease.

I called the Arthritis Foundation that very same week and asked them what resources and groups were available. They told me about a group meeting at the Senior Center in Broken Arrow, Oklahoma. They also sent me free pamphlets on various topics related to managing rheumatoid arthritis and flyers explaining the resources they offered at that time, which included support groups, self-help groups, People with Arthritis Can Exercise (PACE) classes, and a warm water aerobics class then co-sponsored by the Arthritis Foundation and the Young Women's Christian Association (YWCA).

I decided I would first try a support group, which met on a weekly basis. When I first attended the group, I had mixed feelings about it. This was the hardest time for me, as far as the pain and the stiffness were concerned. This was my first attempt to get back into some sort of social group other than church since I had my flare in 1987.

Broken Arrow Support Group

When I attended my first support group meeting, I found the group leader encouraging, and the members supportive. This was

1989, before most of the newer drugs we have now were even conceived of, or researched, or approved for treatment. Many of the older people in this group with RA had extreme debilitation. Many had deformities in their hands and feet. One man's hands were so gnarled, he couldn't tie his shoelaces or button his shirt without assistive devices. Another beautiful middle-aged lady's fingers were so deformed, she had problems holding a pencil or even a cup of coffee. Thus, although the group gave me the feeling that I wasn't alone and let me see people who had much more significant problems than I did, I found it difficult, at age 38, with two young daughters at home, to see what could become my future if this disease were not checked.

Nevertheless, it is ironic that while I was comparing myself to people with significant debilitation, I also found myself in an environment in which I compared myself to those who were much older than I. Yet these seniors could participate in activities that I, at age 38, had been forced to give up because of my illness.

I remember one day at the meeting, as the group leader was discussing some new assistive device, I could hear balls bouncing on the gym floor next door to where our meeting was being held. "Those people are mostly in their sixties and seventies." I thought to myself. "They are doing what I should be able to do. But just the thought of bouncing a basketball makes my hands hurt worse." As the balls continued to bounce against the gym floor, I suddenly felt even more defective than I had before I came to the meeting.

Fortunately, however, I did not give up on the meetings due to this one negative reaction. I stuck it out, and as I attended more of the sessions, I realized I could benefit from the experiences of these brave people in the group who surrounded me. There were people in the group who not only had RA but other types of arthritis, such as severe osteoarthritis, systemic lupus, polymyalgia rheumatica, ankylosing spondylitis, and psoriatic arthritis. Many had discovered ways to deal with the pain, the joint stiffness, and the fatigue that is at times overwhelming for a person with moderate to severe arthritis. Those who don't understand severe arthritis may believe it is just an "old person's disease," which can be managed with a couple of aspirin and slathers of Ben-Gay. However, although osteoarthritis is a common complaint of seniors, many who have autoimmune arthritis become ill at a much younger age. There are even young children who are diagnosed with juvenile arthritis.

Health magazines often display pictures of people with arthritis jumping out of an airplane, skiing down a snowy slope, or running in a marathon. I guess this could be encouraging to many who have the same diagnosis. I can see why such people can be an inspiration to others with arthritis or autoimmune disease.

Nevertheless, I came to be even more inspired by those people in my first support group, who despite severe pain and debilitation, showed up each week with a smile on their faces and shared their small victories in being able to mow their lawn or do woodworking or cook a large meal for their family or sew a button on a shirt. These quiet heroes, who never made the cover of a magazine nor graced the screen of a television set, were the ones who gave me the courage to think that if they could do what they were doing with their severe limitations, then maybe I could go home and care for my two young daughters and still do something positive with my life.

The Magic Triangle

After a few months of meetings, I noticed a curious group dynamic developing. I soon realized that each person who shared at the meetings seemed to feel better at the end of the session. I finally concluded that it was because of three things I saw happening at each session. First, each person was empowered to share his or her greatest frustration or challenge from the week before. Second, as each person shared, the other members would identify with a similar type of problem or provide positive feedback for the member who was sharing; or perhaps another member had found a tip that worked to help with this type of issue. Third, the group leader always ended our meetings with coping skills. We didn't just come in and sit down and start complaining and then go home. If we had done that, everyone would leave with their own problems and with everyone else's.

The group facilitator, who had been trained by the Arthritis Foundation to lead a mutual support group, always gave the group members the opportunity for sharing challenges, but at the same time focused on positive ways to remain active and manage pain despite the disease. Because of this three-tiered format, I found that after a few months, I was learning information to help me cope with the illness and forming bonds with the other group members that gave me the feeling that I was not alone anymore.

About a year after I had been attending this group, the group leader was forced to give up the leadership due to family obligations. She asked me if I would like to facilitate the group after she was gone. A week later I found myself sitting in one of the offices of the local chapter of the Arthritis Foundation, and being handed a loose-leaf binder, filled with information on how to conduct or facilitate a mutual support group. By mutual, I mean a group that is led by someone who has that same type of challenge as the other members in the group. I learned about how a good support group is begun, nurtured, and maintained. The whole process has always reminded me of growing a plant in your garden. You need to know when and where to plant the seed and how to give it the resources it needs to grow and remain a healthy plant. The same is true for a good support group.

Thus, even years before I had reached the Surface and even while I was still floundering in Deep Water myself, I began facilitating groups for the first time. The first group I ever facilitated was my own support group in Broken Arrow.

Swimmers find that by reaching out in front of them and pulling the water to their side, they, themselves, can move forward in the water. I believe that in a similar way, people who reach out to others often begin to make greater progress themselves. Thus, by reaching out and giving of myself to others, I began to regain my own sense of self-worth. I also learned that in the right environment of mutual acceptance and respect, a person who is hurting physically and emotionally can find a way out of fear and isolation, at least temporarily. These first sets of Swim Strokes came while I was still Under the Water myself, but they provided the impetus to get me off the Bottom.

Together

Ugly, aching, emptiness,
Born from common pain,
Mirrored in each eye,
Flows together greedily
From one to heart to another . . .
And we are filled.

(Deboarh Steen, 1992)

Stoic Response Versus Victim Response

After years of facilitating support groups, I was intrigued to witness an extraordinary process of healing that occurred each week. I saw that, in a good support group, two unhealthy extremes of responses to chronic illness could be avoided. I call these two unhelpful responses the "stoic response" and the "victim response."

In my view, both are equally damaging to one's healing process.

In the "stoic response," people in pain are rewarded for stuffing their problems and feelings about those problems. This is the convenient choice for those who fear making others around them uncomfortable by drawing attention to negative circumstances in the "land of ill-health." In the healthy world, there is a pressure, at times, to reinforce this stoic response from people who are hurting. In general, this "no pain/no gain" mentality is appropriate for the athlete or the sports enthusiast in training, whose worst fears center around pulling a hamstring or injuring a knee. The stuffer's theme song is "Laugh and the world laughs with you. Cry and you cry alone."

But for those of us who deal with pain on a daily basis and with symptoms that are confusing and that do not go away, this stuffing response can only increase our dysfunction by increasing our anxiety and depression.

When I worked in the psychiatric hospital, we would routinely see people as inpatients who had stuffed their true feelings for years and had taken care of everyone else around them rather than taking care of themselves. Finally, their emotions had reached a flash point and their suppressed anger exploded into rage or aggression or had turned inward into severe depression with or without thoughts of suicide or suicide attempts.

Thus, I believe one of the primary goals of a good support group is to provide a safe environment in which we all are encouraged to put words to our pain and have that pain validated. I suggest that just by talking about the problem, within a context of mutual sharing and mutual validation, we can look at it more objectively thereby weakening its power over us.

The second unhealthy response, however, lies on the opposite end of the coping spectrum: the "victim response." Although I believe it is important for us to share our problems and feelings in the group, I believe it is equally important for us to avoid embracing the victim role and setting up residence there. This is where the healthy sharing of coping skills and adaptive strategies within the group comes into play.

I believe a good support group is not only a support group, but an education group as well. This group will regularly invite guest speakers who are health professionals or non-professionals who have discovered new ways of dealing with difficult issues to the group to share important and relevant information in the meeting. In this type of group, we all learn these valuable Swim Strokes while we are still at the Bottom of the Pool. However, we must practice our Swimming rather than just bemoaning our Sinking. If we hold on to the anchor of victimhood, that anchor will cause us to drown in self-pity and despair. We will never reach the Top if we don't force ourselves to Push Off from the Bottom.

Arthritis Self-Help Class

A perfect example of a good education group was the Arthritis Self-Help Class, sponsored by the Arthritis Foundation. After I had grown comfortable with facilitating the Broken Arrow group, I was asked if I would like to train to become a Self-Help class instructor. This group met once a week for six weeks. A reasonable fee of fifteen dollars paid for the textbook, which was a manual covering such important and relevant topics as joint protection, pain management, nutrition, exercise, depression and anxiety management, and doctor/patient relationships. The Foundation depended on volunteers, trained by healthcare specialists, who themselves were volunteers, to lead this group.

This was the first opportunity I had to address these topics. By learning how to assist others with information, I gained a wealth of information for myself. I learned, for example, the importance of getting a balance of rest and exercise. I also learned that isolation at home can only increase one's pain levels and depression and that some type of regular or spontaneous or routine socialization, such as attending a support group, having a lunch with a friend, or joining a social club, is an important part of self-care.

I didn't know it at the time, but this training by the Arthritis Foundation for facilitating support groups and leading the Self-Help Class, was a great preparation for what I would be doing later in my school work and in my career. It seemed that the more I shared information with others, the more worthwhile and capable I felt about myself. I found it interesting that I only began to successfully manage my own illness after I had been trained how to help other people manage theirs.

WINSA

Another lesson in Swimming began sometime around 1990, when I and one of my good friends, Barbara, who had ankylosing spondylitis started a new women's support group in Broken Arrow, called WINSA (Women in Need of Support with Arthritis). We formed this group after we noticed how women could benefit from a group especially for them, in which they could discuss how arthritis had affected their relationships. We also organized style shows and luncheons and invited medical professionals to speak at our meetings. I now can see how important this re-launching back out into the community really was for me. In the years to come, the groups I worked with gave me a renewed sense of self-worth, that I had lost during the difficult years after my first onset. I co-facilitated this group with Barbara until 1994.

Our WINSA group even teamed up with the Arthritis Foundation to sponsor a community forum called "Marriage and Arthritis: A Joint Effort." My church at that time, the Garnett Church of Christ in Tulsa, Oklahoma agreed to host this event and to provide the professional videotaping of the meeting. The forum consisted of a group of panelists, which included a rheumatologist, a licensed professional counselor, a registered nurse and biofeedback specialist, who had rheumatoid arthritis herself as well as a daughter with juvenile arthritis, and her husband. The panel answered questions regarding such topics as the following: communicating needs, maintaining intimacy, finding information, setting healthy boundaries, and communicating with doctors.

One of our WINSA members, who seemed to benefit the most from this forum, told us how much it helped her own relationship with her husband – that it helped him better understand what she was going through. Unfortunately, this sweet lady developed lung cancer and passed away not long after she was diagnosed. About two weeks before she passed away, I received a call from her. She told me her counselor told her to call someone who was in pain to encourage that person and that this act of reaching out would strengthen her as well. She told me she wanted to call me to encourage me, because she had benefited so much from the groups I had facilitated. The last thing she said to me was "Debbie, my counselor was right, I really do feel better after calling to encourage you." This was my last conversation with her. In the days following her death, I realized that she, too, had learned her own set of Swim Strokes. By reaching out to me, she was more able to cope with the crushing Waves in her own Deep End of the Pool.

COPING

Another mutual support group, which I facilitated and from which I also gained support myself was called COPING (Christians Overcoming through Prayer and Identifying a Need for God). To start this group, I joined with my friend, Linda. She and I organized this group to provide support to people with any type of chronic illness, including arthritis, heart disease, and cancer. We met once a month and discussed ways to access our Christian faith to help us deal with chronic pain and illness.

One lady in this group, named Vivian, who was also in WINSA, touched my heart in a special way. She had severe arthritis along with a chronic heart condition. She was in extreme pain and had difficulties walking, but she came faithfully to every meeting. One of the ways she helped our group was in giving positive feedback to the other group members. One of her greatest gifts was her ability to sensitively reflect feelings and provide encouragement to someone who was sharing. In addition, she was a fun person to be around. She loved to wear hats. Vivian began the group tradition of wearing hats to our Spring luncheons. The ladies in WINSA and in COPING were inspired to find a beautiful hat to wear each year, but none could compete with the ones Vivian wore. Thus, she inherited the name, "The Hat Lady."

By the time I finished my degree, and around the same time we started COPING, we learned that there were only a few arthritis groups still meeting in the Tulsa area. Thus, around the same time that Linda and I started COPING, we also began an arthritis group in Tulsa, called TEAM (Tulsans Engaged in Arthritis Management). This group, which met twice a month, was designed to serve the needs of people with arthritis, both men and women, in the Tulsa Metropolitan area. This group is still my own arthritis support group today. I'll never forget the amazing transformation I have seen in some of the people in this group.

I never cease to be amazed at how a good group can enhance the healing process. A lady came to our meeting and made a different kind of impression. At the first meetings she attended, she kept telling us she didn't really have time for this group. She said she had numerous projects that were left undone at home and that she needed to be there working on them. Nevertheless, she became one of our most loyal members. She always made us laugh when she wore iridescent colored ribbons woven into her short hair to color coordinate with whatever holiday it was: glittering red for Christmas, twinkling green for St. Patrick's Day, and shimmering pink for Easter. She always brought a sparkle to the group.

One of the advantages of my being in a good support group is the information I have accessed from other members in the group.

One lady I continue to share information with is Linda, my co-facilitator in the COPING and TEAM groups. Although she has lupus, and I have Behcet's, we have many symptoms in common. Like me, Linda has both Raynaud's and Sjogren's and, like me, has a growing list of chemical sensitivities. I have learned through the years of dealing with chronic illness, that an important part of developing Swim Strokes is finding others who are dealing with the same issues you are. At times, when I get extremely frustrated with symptoms or diagnoses that make little sense to me, I have called Linda, and she knows exactly what I'm talking about, since she has more than likely experienced something similar.

Another resource person I went to when I needed support or information about some aspect of arthritis management was Marsha. Marsha was the only person who showed up to our first TEAM meeting. After only a few sessions, our numbers began to grow. When I began my outpatient counseling, Marsha took over the leadership and did a wonderful job facilitating this group. She was the main reason the group has lasted until now. She had RA with multiple overlaps such as Sjogren's and Raynaud's and was a brain cancer survivor.

In the summer of 2014, when my ophthalmologist found I had developed retinal toxicity due to Plaquenil use, he didn't insist that I stop this medication at that time. I didn't know whether I should stop the medication or wait until my doctor insisted it was the right thing to do.

I called Marsha. She told me she had stayed on this medication after the toxicity was first detected, and it left a large hole in the middle of her visual field. She added that the vision loss even continued beyond the time when she stopped the drug. This gave me the information I needed. I immediately stopped taking this medicine. As a result, my visual field loss was minimal compared to Marsha's.

Sadly, in February of this year, Marsha passed away, but I'm certain the group she facilitated for the last ten years, will always remember her love and concern for people in TEAM. We will all miss her dearly. I have no doubt that Marsha's Swim Strokes will leave a wake in all our memories for years to come.

Faith-Based Groups

Another type of group that has helped me in more recent times is my small group or "community group" sponsored by Park Plaza Church of Christ, my current church home. Clem and Kathy Witt, have been our leaders for this group for many years now. Clem was the man who came to pray with me before my orbital cellulitis surgery, mentioned in Chapter Four. This group was my spiritual support group, and these good people prayed for me during both the eye surgery and the "cancer" surgery. I am still a member of this group today, and I love them all. When I can't make the meetings because I'm in a flare, they understand and pray for me. It is important for a person with chronic illness to know that they have a group like this to rely upon in difficult times. My good friends Dorothy and Larry Layman, are both in this group. During the cellulitis emergency, they came to my house and kept my grandkids so that my daughter could be at the hospital with me. Dorothy has been my "rock" for thirty years now. I called both Kathy Witt and Dorothy to pray for me when I was in Houston. They did so, along with numerous other people. Being covered in the prayers of others makes a huge difference in the healing process.

Another faith-based group that has provided support for me is my Heartfelt Group. In the late summer of 2016, right after I was diagnosed with possible ovarian cancer, I received a call from Kathy. She told me that she was organizing a small group made up of Heartfelt Moms, or older women who would agree to be mentors and younger women, Heartfelt Sisters, who would like to be mentored. It was part of a nation-wide program called the Heartfelt Groups. (Kirby, n.d.) Our WINGS or women's ministry at our church was sponsoring this group at Park Plaza.

This was only a few weeks before I was scheduled to go to Houston for my cancer treatment. At first, I told Kathy that I wouldn't be able to do it, because I was getting ready to have surgery. She told me she knew about that, but that I could start the program late. She said she thought it was important for me to be a part of this group and that the group could be a support to me while I was going through this difficult time.

As Kathy continued to encourage me, I knew that God wanted me to do this even if it didn't make any sense to me at that time. I just felt that it was the right thing to do. I finally agreed to join the group. Later when I returned from Houston and was recovering from surgery, this group became a huge source of love and support for me. In fact, we older ladies found that we learned more from the younger women than they learned from us.

I am grateful for all the members of this Heartfelt Group and for my community group, and my church, and all my family and friends who prayed for me during these challenging times. The prayers evidently were answered in a surprising way, when, as mentioned in Chapter Five, the cancer diagnosis was completely reversed. Not only did these groups help me cope with two major life-threatening complications. They also taught me another type of Swim Stroke – learning how to receive support during my most vulnerable times.

I also learned even more Swim Strokes when I found myself facilitating other groups that were not my own support groups, but ones that were part of my assigned responsibility as a professional counselor. I believe that God called me to take the knowledge and experience that I had gained from my own groups, mentioned above, to help people with other types of problems get the support they needed as well. I find it quite interesting how this all came about.

After years of attending and facilitating mutual support groups, I was presented with the opportunity to reconnect with my earlier professional life goals, which I had left behind when I became ill. However, due to chronic pain and fatigue and an illness that continued to wax and wane unpredictably, I believed resuming my high school teaching career was not something I wanted to do, since I had found schools to be one of the most stressful environments in which to work. Nevertheless, God helped me find a new career in which I could bring together all the former skills I had learned both in my bachelor's program, my teacher training, and my work with my mutual support groups. By introducing me to this new and exciting change of direction, God gave me my next set of Swim Strokes – becoming a professional counselor.

Counselor: To Be or Not to Be

One episode that stands out in my mind came when I was having lunch with a friend, Hope Sutherland, who was then the President of the Northeastern Oklahoma Chapter of the Arthritis Foundation. Hope asked me if I had ever considered becoming a counselor. I told her that idea had never crossed my mind. She told me she thought since I had done well facilitating support groups, I would make a good chronic illness counselor.

I honestly was caught off-guard by this question. I realized that I was now over forty years old. Becoming a counselor meant going to graduate school, getting a master's degree in counseling, and then doing supervised work hours to get a state license. Not only that, but since I had my bachelor's in English rather than psychology, I would probably have to take more undergraduate psychology classes before I could even begin my master's work.

When I mentioned all this to her Hope didn't let me off the hook so easily. She acknowledged that it would take a lot of work but insisted that I could do it. She said that by doing so I could, in turn, help a lot of people. I agreed to think about it, but, in all honesty, I filed it away in the back of mind under the category, "Things to Think about but Never Do."

A month or two later, I decided to go to my daughters' school and talk to their counselor about ways I could help them adjust to my chronic health issues. The counselor told me that from what she could tell, the girls were doing just fine. Their grades were good, and they seemed to be adjusting well. Then, a familiar theme began to emerge when she, too, asked me about whether I had ever thought about becoming a counselor.

I was intrigued by this same question coming so closely on the heels of the question Hope had asked me only a short time before. I told her I had no plans for going back to school and that even the thought of doing so was intimidating at my age with all my chronic health issues. She told me she was currently taking classes to earn her master's while working full-time at the school. I thanked her for talking to me and left her office feeling like someone, somewhere must be trying to tell me something. Why was I getting this question now, after years of learning ways to manage a chronic pain condition? My disease was calmer now than it had been earlier, but I still had days when I felt I was running a marathon just to get through them. How could I succeed in getting a master's when I still spent so many days in survival mode? Nevertheless, now that two people had asked me the same question, I decided I had better at least consider the possibility.

In the weeks that followed, while I was sifting through the pros and cons of the idea, something occurred to help make up my mind for me. I received a call from a lady with lupus who had recently attended our support group and who was now threatening to take her own life and that of her children as well. I had no idea exactly what I should do or say, but I knew I had to do something.

I finally got someone to stay with her children while I got her in to see her rheumatologist on an emergency basis. God must have guided me to do this, because, at this time, I had no training in suicide intervention. The rheumatologist found that some of her medications were contributing to the depression. I never saw the lady again, but her doctor and nurse both thanked me later and told me they were glad I had taken her threats seriously. They told me by my getting involved I had most likely saved her life and the lives of her children.

Initially, after this episode, I felt relieved. However, the more I thought about it, the more I realized this lady had needed more than a support group could give her. I also realized that I was not trained to help people the way I wanted to help them. I told myself there was a real need in our community for more people who know firsthand what it's like to live with chronic illness and who also know how to help others in a more professional way.

This incident made me rethink the idea of possibly becoming a counselor. As a support group leader, I could help some people in a very limited way. As a professional counselor, I could help more people who are struggling not only with the chronic medical issues, but with clinical depression as well. This experience came before the phone call from Marvin mentioned in Chapter Four. I was thinking that if this is what God had planned for me, then I wouldn't have to do it on my own strength. He would help me find the way. That same week, I began researching what would be required for me to get a master's in counseling psychology.

School Days

My next group of Swim Strokes (still Under the Water, of course) were made possible when, at age forty-three I decided to give graduate school a try. In 1993, I took the graduate entrance exam and passed it. I then began to work on my 18 hours of pre-requisites before I could be accepted into the Graduate Program. This became the nineties for me: reading, doing research in the library, writing papers, carpooling the girls to activities, studying for exams, and trying my best to learn how to access and run the vintage computer programs for my research.

In 1996, the Surface came a little closer when I was admitted into the Northeastern State University Counseling Psychology Program. I was also learning firsthand how to manage depression, myself, and much about ways to help other people who struggled not only with clinical depression but also a host of other mental disorders such as anxiety, PTSD, and bipolar disorders. I also learned how to diagnose and treat such issues as schizophrenia and OCD and hoarding disorder as well as ways to help patients with sexual abuse and domestic violence histories. During this time of learning and interning, the Swim Strokes became smoother as I made my way upwards to the Top of the Pool.

The Brookhaven Way

By the middle of 1999, I had completed the coursework for the fifty-hour program and was finishing up my thesis, an original research paper on adolescents and depression. In 2000, I began my internship at Brookhaven Psychiatric Hospital in Tulsa, Oklahoma. This was an exciting time for me. I learned how to facilitate therapy groups, take group notes for the patient charts, and assist other therapists in testing procedures whenever I was needed in the behavioral and eating disorders programs. In December of 2001, I completed the fifty-hour master's program and graduated with an MS in Counseling Psychology

This same year, after completing my internship, I was hired as a part-time inpatient therapist at Brookhaven. By this time, I was not only a part-time employee at this psychiatric hospital but was also trying to complete the extra ten hours of coursework necessary to earn an LPC license.

In 2003, I was asked if I wanted to help start the outpatient program at Brookhaven. I jumped at the chance, since this would give me the opportunity to see my own outpatients and have my own office. I worked together with another therapist to get the program up and running. I treasured the time I spent doing individual outpatient therapy.

I was extremely grateful to Brookhaven for allowing me a flexible work schedule. I greatly enjoyed my work and interacting with the other therapists there. More importantly, I found a tremendous amount of satisfaction in being able to help others who were dealing with significant issues and needed skills to cope more successfully. What truly enriched me during this special time of my life was seeing the dramatic transformation that came with the therapeutic process from the first session to the last: a tight, rigid brow relaxing into softness; laughter replacing tears; and, most important of all, the death of "I can't," and the birth of "I can."

After three years working as an outpatient counselor, I at last accumulated enough supervised hours to apply for my professional counselor's license from the State of Oklahoma. All that was standing between me and a license now was the State LPC Exam. I took the test and passed in all sections. Finally, in April of 2007, I became a licensed professional counselor in the State of Oklahoma. This was a huge milestone for me. Getting my master's degree in 2001 and later getting my LPC license in 2007, meant two major life goals accomplished that I, at an earlier time in my life, thought never could happen ever since my first flare.

Individual Therapy

I enjoyed doing individual counseling with my outpatients. This work was quite different from leading support groups. I can still see the faces of these clients and remember their stories of struggling with mental illness, with families and friends who did not understand at all what they were going through, and who judged them for their afflictions. They also struggled against a social paradigm that often blames them for their weakness and questions their faith or spirituality. It isn't as easy to blame a person who has diabetes for having a chemical imbalance due to a diseased pancreas as it is to blame a person with a bipolar disorder who has a chemical imbalance in his brain and nervous system.

To protect the confidentiality of these patients, I cannot describe any particular case. What I can tell you from my experience as a counselor is that there are hurting people all around us. When we go to the store, when we take in a ballgame, when we attend church, we can be certain that someone we meet is hurting either emotionally or physically or both. Many are brave actors, who, perhaps, wear a smile and tell a joke or two, but deep inside they are carrying around a heavy burden of sorrow, guilt, or shame. Many of these patients, coming to me with very different treatment issues, had hit the Bottom themselves. They had no idea how to Push Off again without someone professionally trained to help them. I was so grateful to God that I could be there for them.

In time, I began to think that God was working in my life to help me take the bad things that I had experienced and use them to help others in this way. Now it was not only the support groups anymore, but the clinical populations I worked with, who benefited in some small way from my own experiences. I was amazed that the Swim Strokes process was allowing me to take my own personal pain and turn it into something that was healing for others.

Therapy Groups

After years of doing individual therapy, however, the inflammation in my eyes caused excessive eye fatigue. Having to maintain my patient charts which contained volumes of fine print became a real problem for me. The blurred vision became such a problem I had difficulty driving home at night. I finally discussed this problem with my clinical supervisor. He told me that he could work out an arrangement with our CEO for me to do group therapy only. This would mean that I would have only a minimum of paperwork.

I appreciate my clinical supervisor, Ron Broughton, and Brookhaven Hospital administrators for providing me with a flexible working arrangement. By allowing me to do group sessions only, I could continue working much longer before my retirement than I would have been able to if I had been expected to continue to do individual therapy. I later developed the first group therapy program at Brookhaven Outpatient Services, writing group workbooks and developing psychoeducational materials for groups on anxiety management, depression management, pain and depression management, obsessive-compulsive disorder and hoarding disorder. I believe God wanted me free to work with groups. That is just what happened.

Parkinson Group

While working at Brookhaven, I was asked to organize and facilitate a support and education group co-sponsored by the Parkinson Foundation of Oklahoma. At that time, I knew nothing about Parkinson's disease. However, after meeting with Jim Keating, who was the Founder and Executive Director of the Foundation at that time, Jim provided me with pamphlets filled with information on

Parkinson's. He also helped me promote the group and drove from Oklahoma City to help with several meetings, bringing in speakers who had important information on how to manage this degenerative neurological condition. Parkinson disease (PD), is one of a group of illnesses called motor-system disorders, which occur due to the loss of dopamine in the brain (Parkinson Foundation of Oklahoma, Retrieved, 2017).

Our group, the East Tulsa Parkinson Support Group, started out small at first, but, in time grew to over thirty members. It consisted of people not only from Tulsa, but from other towns in Northeastern Oklahoma. This group was the first group I started as part of my job at Brookhaven.

People in the Parkinson group stand out vividly in my mind. I remember one man in our group who had for years enjoyed fly-fishing. Now, because of shaking hands and poor vision, he was no longer able to tie off a lure. Every time he talked about having to give up this favorite pastime, tears would well up in his eyes.

Another man had loved singing in a barbershop quartet. His Parkinson's had affected his vocal muscles so significantly that he could no longer sing. I also think of the man who had been a rancher for years and had loved hard work and the physically demanding tasks that come with caring for a herd of cattle. Because of Parkinson's, he was finding it harder and harder to do the job he loved to do. There was also a minister who had profound speech and movement disorders with problems swallowing as well. He was the veteran in the group, having lived with Parkinson's longer than any other member. His wife, a constant source of strength to him, was also a member of our group.

Again, I can see the man who had developed such severe shaking and movement disorders that he was told that he had to give up driving a car. For years, he had been driving himself and his mother, who also had Parkinson's. He had a hard time accepting the fact that he could no longer drive. However, this is something that many, if not most, people with Parkinson's face at some time during the progress of their disease.

Loud Crowd

Despite the profound losses experienced by these Parkinson Group members, I also witnessed how these people often found their own set of Swim Strokes, thanks to the services provided by the Parkinson Foundation of Oklahoma. One of the most exciting programs offered by the PFO is the Speak Out and Loud Crowd therapy and group programs that were scouted out and brought to Oklahoma by Jim Keating.

This program is based on the idea that strengthening the vocal muscles with speech therapy, helps a person with Parkinson's talk louder and swallow better and avoid many of the severe choking and food inhalation problems that the illness often causes. This program first offers a series of four sessions of speech therapy provided by a licensed speech therapist, which is then followed up by a group, which continues indefinitely. Insurance and/or Medicare pays for the speech therapy, and the PFO covers the cost of the follow-up groups (Parkinson Foundation of Oklahoma, 2012).

One of the men in our group had severe problems with swallowing when he first came to our group. He was having to eat only liquid or semi-liquids, but nothing solid. "I would give anything just to be able to eat a regular meal with my family," he told us. He later enrolled in the Loud Crowd program. After his specialized speech therapy and lots of practice at home and in the follow-up group, he was again able to eat solid food without the danger of inhaling it. He passed away not too long after this, but, because of Loud Crowd, was able to eat solid food with his family before he passed. His wife continued to come to our group and later became a volunteer for the PFO. Almost every member of our group who had Parkinson's went through this amazing speech therapy program, and most of them experienced an increased ability to talk at a normal volume and swallow food with fewer risks.

Whether an illness is life-threatening or not, it can certainly be life-stealing, because it can dramatically affect the quality of one's life. This is certainly true of Parkinson's. One man joined our group early on. He had worked for an airline company. He had always been extremely active and energetic and was a true leader in everything he did because of his great people skills. I watched as he put his coping skills into action. Bob did it all: exercise, voice therapy, and groups. He was a great help to me, especially in the beginning of our group, because he always seemed to understand how to keep things running – a skill he had used in his career with the airline.

However, despite his commitment to positive management of his condition, the progression of his illness in the last few years became increasingly significant. Although his positive strategies helped him cope in the early days of his illness, his disease was quite progressive, and he began falling repeatedly and eventually required a walker to ambulate. I watched as his wife, who joined our group after her retirement, did everything she could to make life easier for him. Both were dedicated supporters of the group and to me as a group leader.

Unfortunately, he recently passed away due to complications of his Parkinson's disease. I will always miss this good man and consider him a hero in the Parkinson's world, who developed his own set of Swim Strokes. I have no doubt that his illness would have progressed much faster had he not done all he could to Push Off from the Bottom of his own Pool.

Guest Speaker: Another Kind of Voice

One of the guest speakers for our Parkinson group was a lady named Barbara. Barbara is a good friend of mine. She developed early onset Parkinson's in 1989 and still managed to get through nursing school and trained to become a nursing educator as well. She has become a true spokesman for those suffering from this illness. Drawing upon her skills in nursing education, she has a way of explaining the technical aspects of the disease in such a way that makes it easy for people to understand these details.

This lady is a role-model of coping for me. After Barbara learned how much exercise helps Parkinson's, she took up golfing. In addition, she found a way to use her own hand tremors to make beautiful abstract watercolor paintings. She says the more her hand shakes, the more beautiful the painting. Barbara has written her own book about her experiences with Parkinson's, entitled, God, Golf, and Parkinson's (Hogg, 2014). There is little doubt that this courageous lady has developed her own set of Swim Strokes and has kept everyone around her inspired by her sincere faith in God and by her beautiful spirit that refuses to be extinguished by any illness.

In essence, by working with all these different groups, both as a member of the group myself or as a professional facilitator, I have come to realize how important this type of support is for the person dealing with an on-going health challenge. I also learned that by helping others and by accepting help from them, I had more strength to maneuver more successfully through the Cross-Currents of my life on the Deep End of the Pool. I knew if God could help me do this, He could help me make it to the Surface and learn how to breathe the Air once again.

LEARNING TO BREATHE

Nature's Treatment Team

Once I had first pushed off the Bottom of the Pool by selecting my treatment team and achieving a preliminary diagnosis, I found some validity to the myriad of symptoms that, at first, had been so difficult to understand or manage. I also discovered ways to manage the symptoms while grieving the changes caused by the illness. Then, I began Swimming again by replacing the lost parts of my life with new people, goals, and treatments to overcome the depression and rebuild a positive identity. Now it was time to break through to the Surface and learn how to Breathe In life again.

The first way I learned to do this was to learn ways to relax and turn off the stress response. To do this I took advantage of nature's own treatment team – relaxation and exercise. For example, by using relaxation exercises such as body awareness exercises, deep breathing, and visualization, I found that I could decrease the stress chemicals in my blood while also reducing physiological stress symptoms, such as increased heart rate, increased blood pressure, increased respiration, and decreased peripheral circulation. In short, I learned that it was essential for me to find a way to turn off the fight-or-flight response every day, for at least twenty minutes each time, if I wanted to give my body what it needed to heal.

Another way I learned to relax was to exercise. I still do range-of-motion exercises, muscle-stretching exercises, walking, and hula-hooping to help me rid my body of the harmful stress chemicals such as adrenaline, noradrenaline, and cortisol that build up daily. These exercises not only help me remain more flexible, with stronger muscles and bones, but also increase endorphins, the feel-good chemicals that my own body produces naturally. This may be why exercise also has been known to prevent or to decrease depression as well.

Humor is Healing

Another tool that helped my body breathe again was humor. Laughter has been called the best medicine. Dr. Siegel, in his article (Siegel, Laugh! It's Good for Body and Soul, 1993) reveals how laughing is much like an aerobic workout that increases our tolerance for discomfort.

He quotes a research study conducted at Loma Linda University School of Medicine and Public Health, which found out something quite interesting about the healing aspects of humor. In this study, ten medical students were asked to watch a comedy movie, while ten other students were instructed to sit in silence in a room. At the end of a predetermined period, blood samples were taken from both groups, which showed the stress hormone levels of those who watched the funny movie dropped dramatically. He explains that humor can decrease our levels of stress hormones, such as adrenaline and cortisol, which make us prone to disease. He also adds that humor triggers certain infection-fighting antibodies, such as Immunoglobulin A (IgA), which are found in saliva, helping the body fight off infection. (Siegel, 1993)

In the same article above, Siegel tells the story of how humor saved the day. Siegel shares the story of a lady with cancer he saw in a hospital corridor, who was dragging around her chemotherapy pump and complaining. "What's the point of living? I'm always dragging this thing around?" she barked as Dr. Siegel walked by her on his way down the hall. He then quickly retorted, "You must be the Dragon Lady." He says the lady started laughing and couldn't stop. According to Siegel, "She really seemed to enjoy laughing – especially with me, a doctor." He describes how she started cracking jokes with her own doctor, which her doctor at first had trouble understanding, since she had such a hopeless prognosis. Nevertheless, this special lady enjoyed humor so much she didn't quit and later started sending her doctor humor cards every week. Soon the doctor started looking forward to these jokes-by-mail.

Dr. Siegel explains that this new habit of laughing and helping others laugh accomplished much more than helping her distract herself from a difficult prognosis. She used them to help her get closer to her doctor on a human level, and this allowed her to feel more in control of her treatment. The laughter also gave her strength by showing her a new way to look at her illness. It also gave her the strength to fight her cancer. When later her doctors tried to convince her to accept their prediction that she would die at Christmas, she told them, "No, I won't. I work at K-mart and Christmas is our busiest time of year."

At the time Siegel's book was written, this lady was still alive. Siegel believes this was partly because every day she chose to be grateful for what she had that day, rather than regretting what had passed or fearing what may be tomorrow. He says he believes her ability to laugh and enjoy her laughter despite her circumstances is what kept her going. Dr. Siegel insists we all should take a lesson from the Dragon Lady. (Siegel, 1993)

Another example of using humor to help us heal is the story Marvin Phillips shared in his book, Never Lick a Moving Blender (Phillips, 1996). The story, borrowed from a Texas newspaper, appears as the title for his book's chapter two, entitled "Chippie Doesn't Sing Much Anymore." The story recounts the misadventures of a Galveston woman who had a pet parakeet named Chippie. While vacuuming her floors, she decided to vacuum out Chippie's cage. As she was doing so, the phone rang. She then turned to answer it without turning off her vacuum cleaner. Unfortunately, Chippie got sucked in by the machine. The woman dropped the phone immediately, turned off the vacuum cleaner, and opened the canister. There was the little parakeet, feathers flattened against his dirty little body, stunned but alive. She snatched him up and rushed into the bathroom, bird in hand. She held him under the faucet and turned it on full blast. Then she spied the hair dryer. She turned it on to "Hot" and "High." The hair dryer did the trick, but it nearly finished Chippie. The next day a reporter called to find out the status of the bird. "How's your parakeet?" he asked. "Well," answered the woman, "Chippie doesn't sing much anymore. He just sort of sits there and stares." (Phillips, 1996)

I laughed so hard the first time I read this story. On my most challenging days, I think I can relate to how Chippie must have felt. By using humor, we can give ourselves an opportunity to laugh, even in the most difficult times. Susan Minstrey-Wells, in her book, A Delicate Balance/Living Successfully with Chronic Illness, references the success that Norman Cousins, a long-time editor of The Saturday Review, had using humor to fight his ankylosing spondylitis, a degenerative disease of the spine. Wells outlines how Cousins decided to try and use humor to fight his pain in his book, Anatomy of An Illness, in which he explains how, after watching classic episodes of the television show, Candid Camera or Marx Brothers movies, he could achieve a full two hours of pain-free sleep (Wells, 2000).

Dealing with Fears and Worries

Another way I learned to Breathe was to distract myself from fear and worry. At the beginning of my life on the Deep End, my worries were mostly about my health and how I would be able to cope and go on with my life and care for my family within a setting of chronic autoimmune disease. I also worried about whether I would ever get a correct diagnosis or whether I would be able to manage the pain and fatigue. After I started back to school, however, my worries centered more around whether I would make it to class on time or get a paper done by the deadline.

However, later my worries shifted radically and centered around my mom, who had been diagnosed with Alzheimer's disease. I had to be responsible for making all the important decisions about her ongoing care. I also worried about the safety of my oldest daughter who had joined the Navy during wartime and would be stationed in some unknown place in the world as a language inter-preter, and I worried about my youngest daughter who was living in New York City and attending Juilliard right after 9/11. Finally, I worried about whether I would ever get my master's degree and an LPC license.

In time, however, I came to realize that these worries were based on fear, not faith, and did nothing positive for the people I was worried about at that time. Not only that, but I had also learned in my psychological studies that my worrying was not productive and only placed a greater strain on my body, mind, and spirit. If I ever wanted to allow my body to heal, I had to learn how to Breathe out worry and Breathe in life.

Jesus Calling

Come to me and rest. I am all around you, to bless and restore. Breathe Me in with each breath . . . Slow down and cling tightly to My hand. I am teaching you a difficult lesson, learned only by hardship . . . The most persistent choice you face is whether to trust Me or to worry. You will never run out of things to worry about, but you can choose to trust Me no matter what . . . Trust Me though the earth gives way and the mountains fall into the heart of the sea (Young, 2004).

Concerns and Objectives

One coping skill I used to Breathe in life again was to turn my fears and worries into concerns and objectives. I came to see that when I called them my fears and worries, it increased the negative power these problems had to harm me and pull me back to the Bottom of the Pool. However, if I called them my concerns and objectives, it took the power away from the problems and gave more power back to me. For example, when I said to myself, "I'm really worried about my mom's Alzheimer's progression," I was giving the disease more power over me than if I said, "I am concerned about my mom's Alzheimer's progression."

The next step was to move from concerns to objectives. It would go something like this: Concern: "I am concerned about my mom's

Alzheimer's progression;" Objective: "What can I do for her today that will help her the most? I can get her favorite sugar-free candy and take it to her when I see her this afternoon." Thus, with this simple shift of thinking, I was moving my focus away from what I couldn't control to what I could do to help her on this special day of both our lives. The shift was also away from the fears about the future and into the opportunities for blessing her today.

The Two Circles of Control

This process in some way resembles the two circles that Stephen Covey describes, in his book entitled, Seven Habits of Highly Successful People. Covey describes two concentric circles. The outside circle contains all my problems, which Covey calls my Circle of Concern. Within that big circle is a smaller circle, which represents all the problems I can change or control, which Covey calls my Circle of Influence.

He maintains that the more time I spend focusing on the smaller circle (the things I can control) and less time focusing on the area within the circle that falls outside of the smaller circle (the things I cannot control), the larger the smaller circle (the things I can control) will become. In other words, if I spend more time focusing on the part of my problem I can control, the more successful I will be.

Covey insists that proactive people focus their efforts in the Circle of Influence. They work on things they can do something about. The nature of their energy is positive. He says that reactive people, on the other hand, do exactly the opposite. They focus their attention more on the Circle of Concern--on the shortcomings of others, on the crises in their lives, and on problems over which they have no control. This reactive focus results in blaming others for their problems, in aggressive language, and in greater feelings of victimization. Covey concludes that the increased amount of negative energy created by that negative focus, combined with neglect in areas of their lives they could do something about, causes their Circle of Influence to shrink (Covey, 1989).

The Serenity Prayer

This two-circles concept also resembles the ideas represented by the first stanza of The Serenity Prayer, commonly thought to have been written by Reinhold Niebuhr, a theologian, in the late 1930's (Niehbuhr, Retrieved, 2017). The Serenity Prayer, however, involves three circles instead of two. These three areas relate to one's control, to one's responsibility, and to one's evaluation of reality. I learned that I could make changes in each of these areas to greatly decrease my anxiety. This would allow me to drink more deeply from the life-giving oxygen all around me. I learned that when I could successfully apply each section of this beautiful prayer, it was like taking a big, beautiful breath of life.

"God grant me the serenity to accept the things I cannot change . . ."

I soon learned that my need to control everything was irrational and increased my anxiety. This need for control robbed me of my peace and of my positive energy to heal. Releasing the control of my life over to God in those things which I couldn't control, allowed me to take a step beyond letting go of perfectionism and people-pleasing and put God back in the driver's seat of my life again. This release of control also freed me to rest and relax my spiritual muscles so that I could be ready for the second part of the prayer.

"God grant me the courage to change the things I can . . ."

I learned that by letting go of the unchangeable in my life, I had much more strength to change the changeable. This was another way of enlarging Covey's smaller circle. For example, since I could not change or control Mom's Alzheimer's disease, I had to give this over to God. On the good days, when I did this, I had much more energy to spend on thinking of things I could do for her. I was giving up focusing on one circle (the part I couldn't control) to increase my focus in another (the part I could control).

"God grant me the wisdom to know the difference . . ."

In this stage of acceptance, I learned how to stand back and look at my life more objectively. In this stage, I was seeking a balance in my life that avoided the polarized regions of over-functioning (becoming a martyr) and under-functioning (becoming a victim). With this prayer, and with God's help, I learned to achieve a synthesis of the possible and the impossible.

This prayer mirrors the great irony that is described in the first step of the Twelve Steps Program, made famous by Alcoholics Anonymous (Alcoholics Anonymous, Retrieved, 2017) and utilized by other twelve-step groups, including Christian groups such as Celebrate Recovery (Tulsa Christian Counseling, Retrieved, 2017). The first step insists that I can only regain power over the uncontrollable things in my life by acknowledging my powerlessness over them. Thus, by addressing the third part of The Serenity Prayer, I learned to recognize those areas in my life where God expects me to take charge and make the necessary changes to heal my own life and, at the same time, to distinguish them from the areas in my life I need to let God take care of. This, to me, is the most difficult step. I can't say that I have mastered any of these skills, but I do better now than ever before with prayer and with God's help every day.

However, as I approached the Surface of the Pool, I experienced health challenges that threatened to send me back to the Deep Water once again. Although the strategies I have outlined earlier did help me push off from the Bottom and did help me begin to find which way was Up again, these things alone were not, in themselves, sufficient to prevent me from being submerged by the next struggle.

The Serenity Prayer

God, grant me the Serenity
To accept the things I cannot change...
Courage to change the things I can,
And Wisdom to know the difference.

Living one day at a time,
Enjoying one moment at a time,
Accepting hardship as the pathway to peace.
Taking, as He did, this sinful world as it is,
Not as I would have it.
Trusting that He will make all things right
if I surrender to His will.
That I may be reasonably happy in this life,
And supremely happy with Him forever in the next.
Amen.

LEARNING TO FLOAT

Lessons from The Deep

Since my first flare in 1987, my life had drastically changed because of chronic illness. I had been forced to give up earlier life goals but was able to choose and fulfill other goals that God had chosen for me. However, despite these health challenges, God had shown me how to take the scraps of energy and talents that I had left and mold them into something that could benefit others as well as myself.

I had learned much from the people in my support groups and found renewed meaning and purpose in my life by reaching out to others who were hurting both physically and emotionally. I had found that my own personal growth came in part from reaching out to help others. In addition, I had learned that my problems were in many ways small when compared to those of others whom I was honored to meet. I had been privileged to witness the tremendous courage and determination of those in my groups and in my clinical practice.

Moreover, I had finally come to understand the value in sharing my pain in appropriate settings, and found it humbling and amazingly freeing to the soul. I had learned the abundant joy of seeing the love given to others returned to me when I needed it the most. I had learned that in the same way that progress came from reaching out, true inner peace came from reaching Up. By allowing myself to be embraced by this peace, I had found a way out of fear and into a faith – a faith that brought surprising outcomes and yet was, most surprisingly, not dependent upon those outcomes.

Faith Gives It Substance

As mentioned in the Introduction, the flotation device that my mother had given me had not held me up when I jumped off the diving board into the deep water. I had felt betrayed by that ring of plastic. It was not designed to be used for that purpose, but I didn't know it at the time.

Earlier I have shared how other things I had put my faith in had also let me down when I became ill. I could no longer trust in myself alone, in my own energy, in my perfect planning nor even in my increasing knowledge of the disease process alone. Then, too, although the medications and doctors had helped me greatly, there came a time when even these supports were not completely effectual in solving my complex health issues. All these things had proven helpful at times, but when I had become overwhelmed with new symptoms that were confusing and difficult to understand or to treat, these resources, too, allowed me to slip back through the ring into the

Deep Water.

What I found that was much more reliable to hold me up, even in the most difficult of times, was my faith in Jesus Christ. Hebrews 11:1 reads, "Now faith is being sure of what we hope for and certain of what we do not see." Through all the confusion, all the uncertainty, and all the twists and turns of life on the Deep End, my faith in Christ is what led me to the Surface again. It was not until the orbital cellulitis attack that I realized what the light at the Bottom of the Pool really was. I believe it was the Light of Christ's love for me and his promise to be with me no matter what might happen. This was a promise I could only take hold of through faith, and it was only by embracing that faith that I found the peace that surrounded me not only during that episode, but also later during the cancer diagnosis as well.

Wayne Connell, President of "Where is God Ministries," founded WIGM to help believers with chronic illness and pain. In his book, Not by Sight, he recounts how his wife, Sherri, had to give up her career in musical theater after developing multiple sclerosis and Lyme disease (Connell, 2012).

Connell explains one of the fallacies that people with faith often confront. He states that people who have chronic illness are often considered as lacking faith. He insists that the opposite is often the case. Although they are often seen as being unsure of God's power, Wayne says it should be recognized that it takes true faith to keep going through difficult times. He even insists that no faith is stronger than that which continues to remain strong through adversity even when the healing doesn't come. He reminds the reader that many believers who have chronic illness and pain and yet have not been healed, have chosen to praise the Lord even in a setting of chronic pain and illness and an uncertain future.

Finally, he points out that although they have not been healed, they have learned a valuable lesson from their brokenness. "With their wounded bodies and minds, those who are suffering are right where God wants all of us: depending on Him for our every need – and that is living a life of faith" (Connell, 2012). I personally don't believe that God wants us to suffer, but He can help us learn how to grow stronger through that suffering.

One lady, who found that her faith remained strong even when her body failed her is Judy Dillard. Judy was a practical nurse, who developed lupus, which was later complicated by kidney failure and a heart electrical problem, that required her to have a pacemaker implanted in her chest. In her book, The Beauty of Pain, Judy shares that she was at first disheartened when she thought she didn't have enough faith for God to heal her. She says that she tried for a long time to prop up what she considered her weak faith and thought her inability to achieve healing was a failure on her part. "It is as if I envisioned God sticking a 'faith thermometer' in my mouth and waiting for it to reach just the right level so He could heal me," she explains.

She adds that this was a painful period for her until she finally realized that faith is not just asking God to do something for you and expecting him to do it quickly. Judy insists that "faith is the way you live your everyday life, even when healing does not come" (Dillard, 2008).

Another example of tremendous faith within a context of chronic illness and pain is found in the story of Margaret Jean Jones. Margaret had become ill at age seven, when, suddenly her back and arms became paralyzed with no warning. For years, the doctors could not find what was causing the paralysis. A few years after that she lost movement in both of her arms. Finally, just two months short of her eighteenth birthday, the paralysis struck again, first one leg and then the other in less than three months. In a matter of weeks, she was too rigid to sit up in a wheelchair. During this time, she was in excruciating pain.

Later in 1957, she spent eighteen weeks at the National Institute of Health in Bethesda, Maryland, where she had every bone in her body x-rayed and was put on a metabolic diet. She was also put on steroidal medications, which were then still in the experimental stages. At last, the doctors arrived at a diagnosis of fibrodysplasia ossificans progressiva, an extremely rare disease involving a hereditary defect in connective tissue causing a "proliferation of interstitial tissue between muscles, followed by calcification and bone formation." Simply put, her muscles were turning into bone (Jones, 1979).

Since her body now was totally rigid, her mother and her aunt had to take over the responsibility for her daily care. However, her aunt later developed a heart condition and could no longer help, and then her mother was suddenly struck by an acute flare of rheumatoid arthritis, leaving her barely able to walk and with little strength left in her arms and hands. Margaret was forced to enter a nursing home at age twenty-one for six weeks until her father could find someone to come into the home and care for her there.

Since Margaret could not move her neck or back and was forced into lying on her back most of the time, she found a creative way to spy on the world around her. She positioned a hand mirror on the bed table in front of her, and this allowed her to view the room around her and even, when the mirror was strategically placed, through the window to the world outside. Despite her disabling condition, she managed to develop a writing career, having many of her articles published in magazines and writing a regular column for the local newspaper, entitled, Through the Looking Glass. She later wrote about her attitude on healing in her autobiography, entitled, The World in My Mirror, in which she states that she prayed for healing. She adds that when it didn't happen, she doubted her faith until one day she found a quotation by Emerson Fosdick that she insists jumped out of the page and into her mind and heart. "You can't live better by living bitter," Fosdick surmised (Jones, 1979).

Margaret relates how those two words kept rattling around inside her head – "bitter" or "better," She shares with her readers how she believed that God had spoken to her through these two words. She insists that after this experience, she concluded God wanted her to choose the latter word on which to hang her life. She thought God was, in effect, saying to her, "Margaret Jean, you can bemoan your fate, wallow in self-misery and self-pity, or you can start searching for constructive ways to add meaning to the life I have given you."

Margaret says that she no longer obsessed about healing nor did she wait to be healed to carve out a purpose-filled life for herself. She concludes,

> "No matter whether our approach is made on the firm steps of well-being or on the limping feet of affliction – or maybe on the inability to use one's feet at all – just around the corner . . . are unspeakable riches, surprising and fulfilling, for those who put their faith in a God who knows what He is doing" (Jones, 1979).

Lisa Copen is the founder and director of "Rest Ministries," a Christian organization serving millions of people who live with chronic illness. She was diagnosed with rheumatoid arthritis in 1993, and later with fibromyalgia, and has found what she believes is God's purpose for her life--reaching out to others who live with daily pain.

Lisa states in her book, Why Can't I Make People Understand? that she believes Christians with chronic illness are experiencing part of God's refinement process. She adds that although it is painful, through this process, God has hand-picked many who will use their illnesses to glorify Him, in even more amazing ways than He could have used their health. She also states that when one personally shares in Jesus' sufferings, he learns a tremendous lesson about God's character.

She says that she occasionally is confronted by someone who believes that there is a formula of Do's and Don'ts, which this person believes will bring about healing. She adds that when she is confronted by this type of individual, she feels sad for this person. She then explains her reason for this reaction. She insists that if "his faith is in the formulas rather than in the right for God to say 'yes' or 'no' to his healing, he will become disheartened by the fact that he cannot manipulate God with his formulas the way he wants to, and his faith may be weakened by this reality" (Copen, 2005).

Similarly, Deniece Adsit, a cancer survivor, in her book, Lessons from the Journey, explains similar views on her on-going battle with cancer. Denise states that she finally came to realize when she came to the end of her treatment, that no matter what happened to her, this was temporary. She writes in her book that if God had chosen to heal her, it was temporary, because she was not created to live in her body forever. She also insists that if God did not choose to heal her in this life on earth, it was also temporary, because she believes that she was created to live forever with Him -without pain, and without difficulty, and without cancer. She finally concludes, "And anyway I look at it that is a miracle" (Adsit, 2015).

Another lady who has learned to hold on to her faith despite her chronic illness is Barbara Hogg. As mentioned in Chapter Seven, she still struggles with the challenges of Parkinson's disease. Barbara shares her own feelings about her lack of healing when her grandson asked her why God hadn't healed her. She said she told him that at times God plans for us to use our illness to glorify Him. She also said to him that she knew God would heal her in His own time (Hogg, 2014).

As for my own view on healing, I don't believe Jesus' answer one way or the other is necessarily a commentary on the quality of my faith. On the other hand, I believe in the same way that we as humans long for unconditional love, Jesus longs for our unconditional faith – a faith that is not dependent upon our healing, but that stems from an uncompromising trust in the One who heals.

Prayer Holds It Together

I believe it would be extremely difficult for one's faith to hold up under life's pressures without prayer. Prayer allows us to have access to the most powerful force in the universe. Nevertheless, God doesn't always answer our prayers the way we would like for Him to answer them.

Even though I have not always had my prayers for complete healing answered in the way I would have liked, there have been times more recently when I have had my prayers answered in some very amazing ways. I remember the Sunday evening prayer group that was praying for me, at the same time the surgeon called to reverse the diagnosis of Wegener's. Furthermore, the doctors still cannot tell me what happened to the phantom tumor or mass behind my eye that was present on the ultrasound right before they wheeled me into surgery and then just disappeared during my procedure. I believe that was surely an answer to prayer – not only to my prayers, but to the prayers of my friends and family. I also believe the complete change in my tumor pathology report from "cancer" to "benign" was Jesus working and answering prayers of many people, some of whom I didn't even know. I give Jesus the credit for all these incidents, which I believe were miraculous testimonies to the power of prayer.

Perhaps the closest we can come to Christ in prayer is when we are the emptiest and the most dependent upon Him. Lisa Copen describes how she had been praying at church about all her plans that she had for the coming week, and asking God to bless them, then later over-hearing her friend's prayer that said, "It's not what I can do for you, Lord, but what You want to do through me." Lisa said that after hearing this, she changed her approach to prayer dramatically. She began to pray that God would draw her closer to him and let her know His will for her life.

During the two biggest health crises of my life, the orbital cellulitis surgery and the threat of ovarian cancer, mentioned in earlier chapters, I was honored to have others praying for me. Because I knew they were praying, I had firm confidence that all would be well. I didn't know for sure that things would turn out as well as they did, but I trusted that God could make it well, no matter what the outcome.

Prayer did three things for me during these difficult times. First, it gave me a personal connection to Jesus, to ask for a positive resolution to the challenges I was facing. Second, it gave me a network of prayers from others, asking for good outcomes from the surgeries as well as good test results. Third, the simple knowledge that others were praying for me brought me the peace I needed to make it through those uncertain days. I believe that prayer really does hold the fabric of our faith together, reinforcing the warp and weave.

Through our own prayers, we can access that power and that peace that Christ brings to us through our prayers. After living many years submerged on the Deep End of the Pool, I had at last broken through to the Surface and, with the help of faith and prayer, was finally learning how to Float.

Hope Gives It Buoyancy

If faith is the fabric the floatable is made of, and prayer is what holds it together, then hope is the Air that fills it on the inside, allowing it to float on the Surface of the Deep End of the Pool. What keeps that Floatable a Floater and not a Sinker is hope. But what kind of hope am I talking about? I already mentioned one kind of hope in Chapter Seven when I mentioned Dr. Siegel's views on hope in the ultimate cure of one's disease. However, there are other types of hope outside the realm of mental and physical health issues. History has taught us that hope can even be found in seemingly hopeless situations. Dr. Elizabeth Kubler-Ross told her story of her visit to a concentration camp just after its liberation in 1945. A young survivor of Majdanek Concentration Camp told her about how she survived only because of a clerical error.

She and all her family (including her brothers and sisters, her parents and grandparents) had all been sent to the gas chamber. However, she had been the last person to arrive, and since there wasn't room for one more person, the guards had pulled her out. What she had learned later was they had crossed her off the list of the living, and they had never gotten back to her. Because of this technical error, the girl managed to survive on the hope that the camp would be liberated before the guards discovered their mistake, and that is exactly what happened (Kubler-Ross, 1995).

However, there are times when hope does fail to prevent the worst from happening in this life. Nevertheless, even in those situations, hope survives even in the most desolate of places. Dr. Kubler-Ross described what she found in the part of the camp mentioned above, where children were being housed before they died. She said the walls were filled with pictures of butterflies, drawn by these children. "Thousands of children going to the gas chambers, and this is the message they leave behind – a butterfly!" she exclaimed. I personally would like to think that these were, perhaps, symbols of a defiant hope that God gave to these children before they died, an inner awareness that no matter what happened to them at Majdanek, something better was coming (Kubler-Ross, 1995).

Philip Yancey, in his book, Where is God When It Hurts? shares another example of a different type of hope, one directly related to faith. He tells the story of a German prisoner of war, named Jurgen Moltmann, who spent time in prisons in Belgium, Scotland, and England during World War II. This man not only had to live with the normal hardships of prison life, but he had to come to terms with his nation's defeat and then with his learning about the horrible atrocities which had been committed in Germany's name. Moltmann explained that in the prison camps, he had watched how some of his fellow prisoners had given up all hope. He said they "collapsed inwardly" [a great description of depression] and became sick because of it, and some of them even died. He says that what kept him from doing the same thing was his rebirth to new life and to a new hope (Yancey, 1990).

Yancey then explains how that hope for Moltmann was a spiritual hope. Yancey says that Moltmann had taken only two books with him to war: Goethe's poems and the works of Nietzche. Yancey adds that when Moltmann had witnessed the complete dissolution of all the foundations that had supported his life until then, he found a New Testament with the Psalms included, a gift from an army chaplain. He turned to the book of Psalms printed in the appendix and read of a "God who is with those of a broken heart" (Ps. 34:18). He said he turned to this God to help him rediscover his long-lost hope (Yancey, 1990). Moltmann later became a famous Christian theologian and wrote his most famous work, The Theology of Hope.

The difference in this type of Christian hope compared to that mentioned in Chapter Seven is like comparing the power of a backyard amateur telescope to that of the Hubble Space Telescope. Whether a reflector or a refractor, the backyard scope is limited by light pollution and by the clouds and atmosphere, which greatly reduce its ability to reveal a true image of what the universe is really like.

On the other hand, the Hubble Space Telescope, with its huge mirror and its synchronal position in earth's orbit above the clouds and the atmosphere, has revealed galaxies and nebulae never seen before and even allowed us to see into the past by capturing the birth of stars in galaxies millions of light years away. Nevertheless, the hope of the Christian goes even further than revealing the birth of stars and galaxies. It extends into the future to focus on the healing power of our eternal Hope, which is Jesus Christ, and there are no clouds or storms or blinding lights to blur that view.

Robert Schuller wrote and talked much about the power of Christian hope. He was noted for saying to those who were struggling, "God will have the last word, and it will be good." Schuller showed us that these words were true because of the life of one man, Jesus Christ. Schuller points out that Jesus was one of the world's greatest possibility thinkers. He had very little going for him. He belonged to a despised minority. He lived in an occupied country. His hometown was Nazareth, a city with a reputation for being culturally backward and deprived. However, as Schuller also explains, despite his humble beginnings on this earth, Jesus was a man who believed in infinite possibilities. According to Schuller, not only did he believe in positive outcomes; he was willing to make the ultimate sacrifice to prove his positive ideas by dying and rising again. This is the basis of the Christian's hope: Because He lives, things will (not might), but will be better (Schuller, 1985/1986).

Sarah Young has written a daily devotional book entitled, Jesus Calling: Enjoying Peace in His Presence (Young, 2004). Sarah was a Christian counselor and missionary in Japan and Australia who had fought her own health battles with melanoma. Each of the daily messages inspired by scripture work to refocus our thoughts on the peace found in walking step-by-step with Jesus. By doing this, we affirm His good will for our lives and His greater purpose for the world.

Jesus Calling

> . . . Circumstances around you are undulating, and there are treacherous-looking waves in the distance. Fix your eyes on Me, the One who never changes. By the time those waves reach you, they will have shrunk to proportions of my design. I am always beside you, helping you face today's waves . . . I am above all things: your problems, your pain, and the swirling events in this ever-changing world. . . When you feel yourself sinking in the sea of circumstances, Say, "Help me, Jesus." and I will draw you back to me (Young, 2004).

Through modeling the love that Jesus offers to us, we can learn to use our own unique challenges to bring comfort to others who are hurting. The Apostle Paul writes to the Corinthian Church:

> Praise be to the God and father of our Lord Jesus Christ, the father of compassion and the God of all comfort, who comforts us in all our troubles, so that we can comfort those in any trouble with the comfort we ourselves have received from God. For just as the sufferings of Christ flow over into our lives, so also through Christ our comfort overflows... And our hope for you is firm, because we know that just as you share in our sufferings, so also you share in our comfort (II Cor. 1:3-7).

According to Lisa Copen, we don't have to have all the answers about how to comfort people before we share with them. She adds that it's our experience and vulnerability that others find comforting and believable. She states:

> For this journey of chronic illness, most of us would prefer to take along a travel companion who has "been there" rather than a travel agent who has just heard about chronic illness. Your experience will be a great blessing to others who are lost and overwhelmed on this unplanned trip! (Copen, 2005)

Henri Nouwen, a theologian and great writer, explained that

ministers "are called to be the wounded healers, the ones who must not only look after their own wounds, but at the same time be prepared to heal the wounds of others" (Nouwen, 1972).

Nouwen spent the last part of his life attending to the needs of a profoundly disabled man, named Adam. Adam could not speak, could not walk, could not dress himself, could not feed himself and suffered from severe epilepsy and frequent grand mal seizures. When Nouwen was asked why he had left his scholarly career that was so successful to perform such menial tasks for this severely dysfunctional man, Nouwen answered, "I am not giving up anything. It is I, not Adam, who gets the main benefit from our friendship."

He went on to explain that Adam had taught him that "what makes us human is not our minds, but our hearts, not our ability to think, but our ability to love" (Yancey, 1996). According to Nouwen, we are all wounded in some way, but the very act of caring for or trying to bring healing into the lives of others, in turn, brings healing into our own lives as well.

An example of this concept is found, also, in the life story of Margaret Jean Jones. Margaret shares the story of her six weeks in the nursing home, in which she met and became friends with many of the elderly people in the home. She also made a friend of a man named Harvey, who had sustained a brain injury in World War II and now spent most of his time in his wheelchair uttering profanities at the staff.

Something about Margaret's disability, however, seemed to

fascinate Harvey. He started bringing her boxes of chocolate-covered cherries and bits of fruit and nuts, all of which he would place on her tray table. She told him that she would have to wait for a nurse to come to help her with these gifts, because she couldn't get her hand to her mouth.

Harvey started coming to her room three or four times a day to visit her and even laughed and talked to her in words that she gradually learned to decode and understand. She was one of the few people around him who had the empathy and the time to listen to his broken sentences.

When Margaret prepared to leave the nursing home, many of the residents tried to get her to stay. Even the nurses were sad to see her go. "But you can't go home now," they said. "We are just beginning to learn the right way to care for you."

After she did leave, her doctor told her that he had gone to the home a day or so after she left to do his rounds and couldn't find Harvey. Finally, he found him in her old room just sitting in his wheelchair staring at her bed. "You know," he told Margaret, "you were really good for that poor man. I never found him in such a relaxed and happy state of mind in all the time I've been treating him" (Jones, 1979).

This story represents the great irony of the wounded healer. Sometimes the more serious the wounds or debilitation that one experiences, the more comfort that person can bring into the lives of those around her, when her faith is motivated by love for others who are hurting. Whereas prayer holds faith together, love gives our faith a human touch. The only hands that Christ has now to comfort others are those of a person like you or me. The only tears that Christ has now to cry with a grieving widow are our tears. The only arms that Christ has now to comfort a frightened child are our arms. In Margaret's case, she couldn't use her hands or arms to give that kind of comfort. Nevertheless, she found a way to reach out from her rigid body to comfort those around her with a heart that was softened by the love of Christ.

Christ Gives It Perfection

We are told by the writer of Hebrews that we should "fix our eyes on Jesus, the author and perfecter of our faith" (Heb. 12: 2). It is Jesus, then, not we, ourselves, who gives our faith perfection. The writer also explains that Jesus, himself, was "made perfect through suffering" (Heb. 2:10). In II Corinthians, we find that God did not heal Paul, because God's "power was made perfect in [Paul's] weakness" (II Cor. 12: 7-10).

The concept of spiritual paradox is woven throughout the New Testament. To lose one's life is to find it (Mark. 8: 35). The first will be last, and the last will be first. (Matt. 19: 30) Humble yourself, and He will lift you up (James 4:10). Finally, as mentioned above, God's "power is made perfect through weakness" (II Cor. 12:9). These concepts are so radically different than those of the world. The world can understand how God shows His power through healing. But how does God show his power through pain and through weakness? I would answer perhaps through the transformative nature of faith, hope, and love.

I also believe that when we look at our difficulties, our imperfections, and our failures in life, we need to realize that our perspectives are distorted when gazing from this side of eternity. God, on the other hand, can see the bigger picture. Corey ten Boom, a Dutch Christian missionary, who had been arrested for sheltering Jews in her home during the Holocaust, survived the concentration camps. What gave Corrie ten Boom the courage not to give up when she was forced to march from one death camp to another? Or when, long after she was freed from the camps, she became trapped inside a body that, during the last four years of her life, could not speak because of the effects of a devastating stroke? (Ten Boom, 1971) I believe it was her faith in Jesus Christ and that it was Christ, Himself, who perfected her faith in such a way that she could endure whatever life threw at her. Amid her silence, He gave her a powerful voice that continues, even today, long after her death, to speak out to a new generation from the pages of her writings. Corrie shared in her speeches and writings that she failed when she tried to overcome her pain and her difficult circumstances on her own strength and power. She insisted that she needed the power of Jesus Christ, Himself, and of His Holy Spirit to help her overcome (Vision Video, 2013).

I have found this to be true in my own life. Every time that I have relied on my own wisdom or strength alone to get me through the most difficult times, I have become overwhelmed. I personally believe that all our attempts at rising above our problems are intrinsically flawed, because we are only humans. As a Christian, however, I believe that these attempts are made perfect by the intervention and suffering of Jesus Christ. The comfort for the Christian comes not from any hope the world has to offer us. It comes, rather, from the story of the Cross--a story that begins with pain and suffering and that ends with eternal and immeasurable . . . Comfort. As Philip Yancey states in his book, The Jesus I Never Knew,

> For proof, look at the cross... the fatally wounded healer came back on Easter, the day that gives a sneak preview of how all history will look from the vantage point of eternity, when every scar, every hurt, every disappointment will be seen in a different light... The disciples who lived through both Friday and Sunday... had learned that when God seems the most absent he may be the closest of all, when God looks the most powerless he may be the most powerful, when God looks the most dead he may be coming back to life. They had learned never to count God out (Yancey, 1995).

A Ring of Life

Chronic illness had sent me to the bottom of the Deep End of the Pool. However, with the help of my doctors and my friends, I had found Swim Strokes that helped me make it back towards the Surface again. Now, I am convinced that God has provided me with a much more reliable Flotation Device, made sturdy through faith, sewn together with prayer, filled to reliable buoyancy with hope, and given comfort through love--a Ring of Life made perfect by Christ, through His death on the cross. I am confident and find true inner peace in the thought that this Ring of Life can, along with His divine help, hold me up through whatever comes next in my ever-changing and unpredictable Life on the Deep End.

Notes

CHAPTER 6

Zeis, Joanne. (2015). *Behcet's Disease*. Dulles, Virginia: Mercury Learning and Info.

Register, Cheri. (1987). *The Chronic Illness Experience: Embracing the Imperfect Life*. Center City, Minnesota: Hazelden.

Shomon, Mary J. (2002). *Living Well with Autoimmune Disease: What Your Doctor Doesn't Tell You that You Need to Know*. New York: Collins.

Baron-Faust, Rita. and Jill. P. Buyon, M.D. (2002). *The Autoimmune Connection: Essential Information for Women on Getting on with Your Life*. New York McGraw-Hill.

Bagley, Cassandra. (2009, Feb. 15). *Multiple Sclerosis and Connective Tissue Diseases*. Retrieved from articledoctor.com: http://www.article.com/diseases-multiple-sclerosis/multiple-sclerosis-and-connective-tissue-diseases-1243

Fremes, Ruth, M. A. and Nancy Carterton, M.D. F.A.C.R. (2003). *A Body Out of Balance: Understanding and Treating Sjogren's Syndrome*. New York: Avery.

Kavanaugh, R. M. (2017, December 20). *Arthritis with Normal Blood Tests? Why not . . .* Retrieved from ronakavanagh.ie/blog:http://www.ronakavanagh.ie/blog/arhtritis-with-normal-blood-tests-why-not/

Rodriguez, D. (2012, September 6). *Tests for Diagnosing Arthritis*. Retrieved from everydayhealth,com:http://www.everydayhealth.com/arthritis/diagnostic-tools-imaging-tests.aspx

Hua, C. et. al (2017). *Diagnosis, Prognosis, and Classification of Early Arthritis: Results of a Systematic Review Informing the 2016 Update of the EULAR Recommendations for the Management of Early Arthritis*. RMD, p. 406.

Vasconcelos, C. (2015, December). *Opportunistic infections and autoimmune diseases*. Retrievedresearchgate.net: https//www.researchgate.net/publication/282596878_Infections_and_Autoimmune_Diseases

Kahan, A., et al. (1992). *Abnormalties of T lymphocytesubsets in Behcet's disease demonstrated with anti-CD5RA and anti-CD29 monoclonal antibodies*. Rheumatology, 742-6.

Lim, S.,et al. (1983). *Abnormalities of T-cell subsets in Behcet's syndrome*. Achives of Dermatology, 307-10.

Dunkin, Mary A. (Retrieved, 2017, Sept. 7). *More Than Just Joints: How Rheumatoid Arthritis Affects the Rest of Your Body*. Retrieved from arthritis.org: http://www.arthritis.org/about-arthritis/types/rheumatoid-arthritis/articles/rheumatoid-arthritis-affects-body.php

Hansen, Mark S., M.D. and Stefanie G. Schuman, M.D. (2011, June). *Opthalmic Pearls: Hydroxychloroquine-Induced Retinal Toxicity.* Retrieved from aao.org.: https://www.aao.org/eyenet/article/hydroxychloro-quine-induced-retinal-toxicity

Ruffing, V. (2016, January 12). *Side-effects of biologic medications.* Retrieved from hopkinsarthritis.org: http://www.hopkinsarthritis.org/arthritis-news/side-effects-of-biologic-medications/

National Institute on Drug Abuse. (Retrieved 2017, August 26). *Opioids: Brief Description.* Retrieved from drugabuse.gov: http://www.dru-gabuse.gov/drugs-abuse/opioids

Brown, RT, et al. (2006). *Adverse effects and cognitive function among primary care patients taking opioids for chronic   nonmalignant pain.* Journal of Opioid Management, 137-146.

Barg, Jacob, et al. (1993, December 31). *Brain Research: Opioid Receptor Density in Alzheimer, Amygdala, and Putamen.* Retrieved from sciencedirect.-com: http://www.sciencedirect.com/science/article/pii/00689939391155L

CHAPTER 7

WebMd. (Retrieved 2017, January 26). *Depression Caused by Chronic Illness.* Retrieved from www.webmd.com:depression/depression-caused-chronic-illness#1

Sveilich, Carol. M. A. (2005). *Just fine: Unmasking Concealed Chronic Illness and Pain.* Austin, Texas: Avid Reader Press.

National Institute of Mental Health. (Oct. 2016). *Depression: Overview.* Retrieved from nimh.nih.gov: https://www.nimh.nih.gov/health/topics/depression/index.shtml

Kubler-Ross, Elizabeth. (1969). *On Death and Dying.* [New York] McMillan.

Kubler-Ross, E. M. (1995). *Interviews with People Who Make a Difference: On Death and Dying.* (D. Redwood, Interviewer).

McIntyre, Bruce. (2012). *Graceful Transitions: An Inspirational Guide for family Caregivers and Care Receivers.* Edmond, Oklahoma: Rabbit Ranch Press.

Donoghue, Paul J., Ph.D. and Mary E. Siegel, Ph.D. (2000). *Sick and tired of Feeling Sick and Tired: Living with Invisible Chronic Illness.* New York: Norton & Co.

Lemelson-MIT Program. (Retrieved 2017, Aug. 29). Chester R. Carlson: *The Photocopier.*

Hartwell, Lori. (2002). *Chronically Happy: Joyful Living in Spite of Chronic Illness.* San Francisco: Poetic Media Press.

Siegel, Bernie M. D. (1993) "*Laugh! It's Good for Body and Soul.*" First Magazine, 33-35.

Yancey, Philip. (1990). *Where Is God When It Hurts?* Grand Rapids, Michigan: Zondervan.

CHAPTER 8

Parkinson Foundation of Oklahoma. (Retrieved 2017, Aug. 29). *What is Parkinson's?* Retrieved from parkinsonoklahoma.com: http://parkinsonoklahoma.com/parkinsons-disease

Hogg, Barbara. (2014). *God, Golf, and Parkinson's.* Bloomington, Indiana: Crossbooks.

CHAPTER 9

Mayo Clinic Staff. (2014, Oct. 10). *Depression and Anxiety: Exercise Eases Symptoms.* Retrieved from mayoclinic.org: http://www.mayoclinic.org/diseases-conditions/depression/in-depth/depression-and-exercise/art-20046495

Siegel, Bernie M. D. (1993) *Laugh! It's Good for Body and Soul.* First Magazine, 33-35.

Phillips, Marvin. (1996) *Never Lick a Moving Blender.* West Monroe, Louisiana: Howard Pub. Co.

Wells, Susan M. (2000). *A Delicate Balance: Living Successfully with Chronic Illness.* Cambridge, Massachusetts: De Capo Press.

Covey, Stephen R. (1989). *The Seven Habits of Highly Successfully People.* New York: Simon & Schuster.

Niebuhr, Reinhold. (Retrieved 2017, Aug. 29). *The Serenity Prayer.* Retrieved from prayerfoundation.org: http://prayerfoundation.org/dailyoffice/serenity-prayer-full-version.htm

Alcoholics Anonymous. (Retrieved, 2017, Aug. 29). *Welcome to Alcoholics Anonymous.* Retrieved from aa.org: https://www.aa.org

Tulsa Christian Counseling. (retrieved 2017, Aug. 29). *Tulsa Christian Counseling Directory: Tulsa Celebrate Recovery.* Retrieved from tulsachristiancounseling.org: http://www.tulsachristiancounseling.org/tulsa-celebrate-recovery

CHAPTER 10

Connell, Wayne. (2012). *Not by Sight.* Parker, Colorado: Where is God Ministries.

Dilliard, Judy. (2008). *The Beauty of Pain.* Denver, Colorado: Outskirts Press.

Jones, Margaret J. (1979). *The World in My Mirror.* Nashville, Tennessee: Abingdon.

Copen, Lisa. (2005). *Why Can't I Make People Understand?* Discovering the Validation Those with Chronic Illness Seek and Why. San Diego, California: Rest Ministries.

Adsit, Deniece. (2015). *Lessons from the Journey.* Tulsa, Oklahoma: Heartsong Press.

Hogg, Barbara. (2014). *God, Golf, and Parkinson's*. Bloomington, Indiana: Crossbooks.

Kubler-Ross, Elizabeth. (1969). *On Death and Dying*. [New York] McMillan.

Kubler-Ross, Elizabeth. (1995). *Interviews with People Who Make a Difference: On Death and Dying*. (D. Redwood, Interviewer).

Yancey, Philip. (1990). *Where Is God When It Hurts?* Grand Rapids, Michigan: Zondervan.

Psalms 34:18. (n.d.). *In The Holy Bible* (New International Version). Grand Rapids, Michigan: Zondervan.

Schuller, Robert. (1985/1986). *The Inspirational Writings of Robert Schuller: The Be-Happy Attitudes/Be Happy You are Loved*. New York: Harper Perennial.

Young, Sarah. (2004). *Jesus is Calling: Enjoying Peace in His Presence*. Nashville, Tennesse: Thomas Nelson.

Nouwen, Henri J. (1972). *The Wounded Healer*. New York: Image Doubleday.

Yancey, Philip. (1996, Dec.9). *Yancey: The Holy Inefficiency of Nouwen*. Retrieved from christianitytoday.com: http://www.christianitytoday.com/ct/1996/december9/6te08o.html?start=1

Heb. 12:2, 2:10. (n.d.). *The Holy Bible* (New International Version). Grand Rapids, Michigan: Zondervan.

II Cor. 12:7-10. (n.d.). *The Holy Bible* (New International Version). Grand Rapids, Michigan: Zondervan

Mark 8:35. (n.d.). *The Holy Bible* (New International Version). Grand Rapids, Michigan: Zondervan

Matt. 19:30. (n.d.). *The Holy Bible* (New International Version). Grand Rapids, Michigan: Zondervan

James 4:10. (n.d.). *The Holy Bible* (New International Version). Grand Rapids, Michigan: Zondervan

Vision Video. (2013). *Corrie ten Boom: A Faith Undefeated*. (C.T. Boom, Performer) DVD.

Resources

General Medical Information

American Medical Association (AMA): www.ama.org

Mayo Clinic: www.mayoclinic.org

Medscape: www.medscape.com (clear, easy-to-understand medical information)

National Institutes of Health (NIH): www.niaid.nih.gov

PubMed: www.pubmed.com (peer-reviewed journals on medical topics)

Arthritis and Arthritis-Related Conditions

American Association for Repetitive Motion Syndrome (ARMS): www.certifiedpst.com/arms

American Autoimmune Related Disease Association (AARDA): www.aarda.org

American Behcet's Disease Association (ABDA): www.behcets.-com

American College of Rheumatology: www.rheumatology.org

American Fibromyalgia Association: www.afsafund.org

American Juvenile Arthritis Association: www.juvenilearthritis.org/communities/children-young-adaHS.asp

Arthritis Foundation: www.arthritis.org

Chron's and Colitis Foundation of America: www.ccfa.org

Chronic Fatigue and Immune Dysfunction Syndrome Association of America: www.cfids.org

Fibromyalgia Network: www.fmnetnews.com

The Lupus Foundation of America, Inc.: www.lupus.org

Lyme Disease Foundation: www.lyme.org

National Institute of Arthritis, Musculoskeletal and Skin Diseases (NIAMS): www.niams.nih.gov

National Osteoporosis Foundation: www.nof.org

Raynaud's Association: www.raynauds.org

Reflex Sympathetic Dystrophy Syndrome Association: www.rs-d.org

The Scleroderma Foundation: www.scleroderma.org

Sjogren's Syndrome Foundation: www.sjogrens.org

Spondylitis Association of America: www.spondylitis.org

Wegener's Granulomatosis: www.arthritis.org/about-arthritis/types/wegeners-granulomatosis

Autoimmune Disease (General)

American Autoimmune Related Disease Association (AARDA): www.aarda.org

Behcet's Disease

American Academy of Dermatology: www.aad.org

American Academy of Ophthalmology: www.aao.org

American Autoimmune Related Disease Association (AARDA):
www.aarda.org

American Behcet's Disease Association (ABDA): www.behcets.-
com

American College of Rheumatology: www.rheumatology.org

Arthritis Foundation: www.arthritis.org

American Ophthalmological Society: www.aosonline.org

Dean McGee Eye Institute: www.dmei.org

National Eye Institute: www.nei.nih.gov

National Organization for Rare Disorders (NORD):
www.rarediseases.org

Cancer

American Cancer Society: www.cancer.org

The University of Texas--MD Anderson Cancer Institute:
www.mdanderson.org

Diabetes

American Association of Clinical Endocrinologists: www.aace.-
com

American Diabetes Association: www.diabetes.org

The Endocrine Society: www.endo-society.org

Gastroenterological Issues

American Gastroenterological Association: www.gastro.org
Celiac Disease Foundation: www.celiac.org
Crohn's and Colitis Foundation of America: www.ccfa.org

Heart and Lung Issues

American Heart Association: www.americanheart.org
American Lung Association: www.lungusa.com
National Heart, Lung, and Blood Disease Institute:
    www.nhlbi.nih.gov

Physical Disabilities- Support

The Center for Individuals with Physical Challenges: www.tul-
    sacenter.org

Urological Issues

American Urological Association: www.auanet.org
International Continence Society: www.ics.org
Interstitial Cystitis Association: www.ichelp.org

Neurological Issues

The ALS Association: www.alsa.org

Alzheimer's Association: www.alz.org

American Academy of Neurology: www.aan.com

American Parkinson's Disease Association: www.apdaparkin-son.org

Myasthenia Gravis Association: www.mgakc.org

Myasthenia Gravis Foundation of America: www.myastheni-a.org

Multiple Sclerosis Association of America: www.mymsaa.org

Multiple Sclerosis Foundation.: www.msfocus.org

National Institute of Neurological Disorders and Stroke: www.ninds.nih.gov

National Multiple Sclerosis Society: www.nmss.org

NIH Neurological Institute: www.ninds.nih.gov

Parkinson Foundation of Oklahoma: www.parkinsonokla-homa.com

Parkinson Voice Project (Loud Crowd): www.parkinsonvoice-project.org/LoudCrowd

Pain Management

American Academy of Pain Management: www.aapainman-age.org

American Chronic Pain Association: www.theacpa.org

We Appreciate Reviews

If you enjoy this *Inkception Books* product, please consider writing a review and posting it to any site where *Inkception Books* are sold. This gets the word out about our products. In appreciation for any reviews we receive on this product, you can receive a one dollar rebate on any *Inkception Books* product. Just email inkceptionbooks@gmail.com with a link to the review you gave, and a copy of the receipt for the product you would like the rebate on. Thanks very much for your continued support of our authors!

Made in the USA
Columbia, SC
17 June 2018